The Daring Female's
Guide to Ecstatic Living

The Daring Female's Guide to Ecstatic Living

30 Dares for a More Gutsy

and Fulfilling Life

NATASHA KOGAN

New York

Library of Congress Cataloging-in-Publication Data

Kogan, Natasha.
The daring female's guide to ecstatic living : 30 dares for a
more gutsy and fulfilling life /
Natasha Kogan.—1st ed.
p.   cm.
Includes bibliographical references.
ISBN 1-4013-0790-6 (alk. paper)
1. Women—Psychology.   2. Risk-taking (Psychology)
3. Self-realization in women.   I. Title.

HQ1206.K56 2006
646.7'0082—dc22   2005047168

Book design by Nicola Ferguson

Hyperion books are available for special promotions and
premiums. For details contact Michael Rentas, Assistant
Director, Inventory Operations, Hyperion,
77 West 66th Street, 11th floor, New York, New York 10023,
or call 212-456-0133.

FIRST EDITION

1   3   5   9   10   8   6   4   2

For my mom and dad, who took on the biggest dare of their lives so that I could live in a place that gave me the freedom to take on my own. You are my heroes.

Contents

Daring Female: A gutsy, passionate, and willful woman who isn't afraid to take risks, chase her dreams, explore new experiences, express her creativity, push her own boundaries, and speak her mind. (Oh, and she doesn't mind embarrassing herself once in a while and having a good laugh about it!)

Introduction

(or Why I Wrote This Book)

A few years ago, I started a publishing company with my husband. We were young, knew absolutely nothing about publishing, and didn't have mountains (or even a good-size pile) of cash to start a business. But we had an idea for a book series, an obsessive love for books, and a lot of naiveté, so we did it. As we struggled to get our publishing baby on its feet, a friend asked me if I was at all scared to do what we were doing. Scared of sinking our life savings into a start-up publishing business that had to compete with publishing giants from an office in our one-bedroom apartment? Nah!

Well, of course I was. I was scared to death, actually, of everything, from losing our savings (the down payment for a house we were hoping to buy soon) to failing to achieve our dream and everything in between. In a moment of weakness, I even wrote out the pros and cons of starting a publishing company, given our lack of knowledge, resources, and the "Wow! How can I not be intimidated by this" figure of 70,000 books published every year and just a few succeeding. There were more cons than pros.

I dared myself to do it anyway—to chase my dream of starting my own company and to beat the odds. (I was lucky that my husband was a willing partner in crime.) I knew that I could always think of a hundred reasons why it would be too difficult to do or too impossible to accomplish. But what would I be left with if I didn't take this risk? A safe, stable life filled with regret, boredom, and endless "woulda/coulda/shoulda." I couldn't think of anything scarier than that, so I dared myself not to be intimidated and to dive headfirst into the world of publishing.

I could write a whole book to tell you about our publishing successes, and a much longer one about our struggles and mistakes, some of which were so naive we now laugh about them. But that's almost irrelevant. What matters more than anything else is that every single day I am pursuing one of my life goals—to run my own company—and I'm feeling more daring and gutsy than I ever have before. Is it a challenge? No doubt. Are there days when I'm exhausted or frustrated and wonder how long we can keep this going? Definitely. Is it worth it? YES!

Starting a company was one of the most difficult things I've ever done but to be honest with you, I'm somewhat addicted to risks, creative challenges, life detours, and anything else that makes life more interesting. The moment I feel settled or sense that my life is flowing along smoothly, I dare myself to do something—change my routine, take a risk, or simply take on a new creative project. That first step—the DARE—is the ultra-important one we all need to take to get the greatest enjoyment, fulfillment, and excitement out of every part of our lives. To really *live* we've got to dare ourselves to DO things—change our routines, take risks, explore new ideas, and experience as many different facets of life as possible. And what I like about a dare is its surprise and inevitability. As in Truth or Dare, the game many of us played as teenagers, we don't know exactly what each dare will be like or how it will turn out, but there's no going back once we've dared ourselves to do something. And ultimately, whether we succeed in each of our dares isn't really that important, because even failed attempts invigorate us, teach us something new, and most of all, make us feel like confident and gutsy Daring Females ready to take on the world.

When I was thinking about writing this book I jotted down some of the things I've achieved in my life. Without fail, each one began as a dare to myself.

DARE 1: Too Old to Lose My Accent

When I was fourteen, my family emigrated from Russia to the United States. Talk about a shock! For a while there I didn't think that I was ever going to find my place in this new world, but I decided to at least try. My first order of business was learning to speak English better than I could after my few years of classes in Russia. I desperately wanted to sound like every other American teenager—Samantha on *Who's the Boss?* was my idol (laugh if you like). Everyone told me that I had started too late to lose my accent completely, but I didn't care: I wanted this so much that I dared myself to try and make it happen. I made an effort to speak only English, which drove my parents crazy, since they were just learning the language themselves. I spent most of my free time after school watching TV and imitating the sounds I heard, looked up hundreds of words in the dictionary, and wrote down and practiced the words that gave me the most trouble, often spending hours repeating them. I poured every ounce of energy I had into trying to learn to speak English like a real American. It took me years—years filled with countless embarrassing mistakes—and many times I nearly lost hope, but if you heard me today, you'd think that I sounded like a regular New Yorker—but without a New York accent!

DARE 2: MBAs Only, Please!

After graduating from college, I went to work for a big-name consulting company in New York. According to numerous career counselors, this company was not a place where many grads from a small liberal arts school like Wesleyan had landed a job. But I wanted to get a taste of the business world and to do it from New York, so I dared myself to apply and compete with top grads from all across the country. I trembled between my interviews and had to go to the bathroom to catch my breath, but I managed to put my fears aside, and months later I moved to New York to join the firm.

DARE 3: You're Giving Up THAT Job?

Several years later I realized that what I really wanted to do was work with small companies and maybe run one of my own someday. I was petrified about giving up my secure job and the nice paycheck and the perks that came with it. To top it off, my parents, friends, and colleagues all thought I was completely insane for leaving such a great job. But I woke up one morning and realized that if I didn't leave at that point, I might not ever leave and take the chance to go after what I really wanted out of life. I dared myself not to be intimidated and spent the next few years helping small businesses grow. Some of the companies I worked with made it, and being part of their success was exhilarating. Some of them failed and taught me many, often painful lessons. Despite the ups and downs, I was out there doing what I wanted, taking risks and living my life to the fullest, and nothing is more exhilarating than that.

DARE 4: You Can't Start a Business (In Your Apartment)

The itch to create my own product from the ground up just wouldn't go away, so I decided to do it by starting a publishing company. I didn't know a lot about what it would take to get the company going, how much time, effort, and money we'd have to spend just to get started, or how difficult it would be to compete with the thousands of titles published by giant companies with millions of dollars in marketing budgets. I consider myself lucky, in a sense, not to have known too much in the beginning or the prospect might've seemed too difficult. I knew enough to make me nervous, but I went for it anyway. I figured that not to attempt this life goal would be worse than trying and failing. It's still a fight every day, and there are days when it becomes more of a fight than I ever bargained for. Yet when I consider the books we've brought to life and all that we've created from absolutely nothing, I feel I can do pretty much anything.

DARE 5: Only Experienced Authors Get Published

Which brings me to my latest dare: to write this book and get it published. I've attempted to publish some of my writing before, each time collecting dozens of rejection letters of the "Thanks but it's not for us" variety. Endless rejection was brutal and intimidating. On top of this, I read dozens of articles about how difficult it is for first-time authors to get published, and dozens more about how it's impossible to find either an agent or a publisher. I heard stories from authors who spent a year writing their book and five years trying to find someone who'd take a chance and publish it. Talk about too much daunting information, this was it. But becoming an author had been on my Life Wish List a long time, so I dared myself to take a chance and give the publishing world all I had.

I decided to write this book to share with you one simple idea that I've learned through my own experiences:

To get the most out of your life,
you have to dare yourself to do it.

Whether you're reading this because you feel your life isn't going in the right direction because you've had a terrible day at work, or because you need a slight kick in the you-know-what to do more with your life, I dare you to use this book as a springboard to launch yourself into a life that's more passionate, interesting, and fun. Realize that you have an amazing power—the ability to grab life by the horns and get from it a tremendous amount of satisfaction, fulfillment, and joy.

Most importantly, dare yourself to be a Daring Female and do something with that power! Dare yourself to live with passion and gusto, and find the guts to go after what matters to you—today, right now, this moment. Whether it's overcoming a great challenge, taking a risk, trying something completely new, or simply making each day more enjoyable and fulfilling, the first step is to dare yourself to do it. This is your life and no one else can take that step for you—so dig deep, find your inner Daring Female, and go for it! So how about it?

Thanks for giving this book a shot,

Natasha

Your loyal Daring Female

Bring on the Dares

(or How to Use This Book)

I didn't conceive of this book as a detailed road map for finding your inner Daring Female. If you had the urge to pick it up or flip through it, then the Daring Female is within you already, and a Daring Female is too strong-willed to follow a plan created by someone else. So instead, use this book as a resource filled with ideas, reflections, and inspirations for becoming your own version of a Daring Female. Browse the contents page and pick a dare that appeals to you. Read the book backwards. If you need to infuse your life with more joy and laughter, read the dares in the "Laugh a Little, Live a Lot" section first; if you're facing a challenge in your life, check out the dares in the section called "Have No Fear."

How you read this book is your call. I ask of you only one thing: Take on at least one dare that you find in it. You'll never know how great it feels unless you try and I hope that as you read, you'll find enough reasons to give it a shot.

Five Things to Do Before You Start the Search for Your Inner Daring Female

1. Give yourself a chance to change.
2. Remember that being wrong can feel absolutely wonderful.
3. Banish your inner perfectionist.
4. Turn up your gutsy energy as high as it will go.
5. Get ready to be surprised!

Daily
Daring
Habits

D F You might think that to be a Daring Female you have to go bungee jumping or drive around in a red convertible, rock 'n' roll tunes blaring. I couldn't disagree more. I mean, if conquering your fear of heights or exchanging your blend-in image for one that's more fun and in-your-face is something you're after, go for it. But a true Daring Female doesn't need to turn her life upside down to be daring. Instead, she infuses every day with a healthy dose of Daring Female attitude, pouring it into even the most mundane of activities. So don't wait for some special time to practice your Daring Female skills; make them part of your daily life. To get you going, here are a few Daring Female Daily Habits to spice up your life and to give you the tools to do with it whatever your heart desires.

Dare to Find What Makes You Ecstatic, and Do It for at Least Ten Minutes a Day

DARE-METER

Daring   Ultra Daring   Ultra-Gutsy Daring

Happiness is not something you get, but something you do.
—MARCELENE COX, WRITER

I remember one particular day when I got to work and couldn't muster the mental energy or motivation to get cracking on my ever-long to-do list. I didn't hate my job—in fact, some days it was actually pretty energizing—but it would be a stretch to say that I was passionate about it. But on this day it was much, much worse—I looked at my e-mail in-box and felt utterly unable to read or respond to any messages.

I couldn't very well just leave, nor could I just sit there and do nothing, so I decided to spend a few minutes warming up to my day by doing something that I knew would make me happy: working up a few ideas for a book that someday I wanted to write. Books and anything remotely related to books has long been one of my obsessive passions, that special kind that always makes me feel invigorated and excited and ready to conquer the world. I took out my Book Ideas Journal (yes, I actually keep one of those) and spent the next few minutes—okay, maybe more than a few— dreaming up new book concepts. I was in heaven. And to my surprise, when I was interrupted with a phone call, I was much more willing to get back to my daily world of financial models and impatient clients.

Dare to find something that makes you utterly ecstatic and do it for at least ten minutes a day! No, it won't solve all of your problems, bring you eternal happiness, or lead to world peace. But it will definitely, absolutely, no doubt make your days have a more positive slant, inspire you to remember what makes you happy, and give you that necessary life-energy shot in the arm. Our lives are filled with so much "I should/I must/I have to" that sometimes we forget to spend time doing things we really enjoy. I dare you to remember what those things are and to find time to enjoy them.

And don't dare use the "I'm too busy!" excuse. Most of us lead busy lives, and you might think you can't squeeze ten minutes out of your day to spend doing what you want.

But those ten minutes are there somewhere; with some organization you will find them, and probably more than just ten. Send one less e-mail, spend less time on the phone, wake up ten minutes earlier, but do whatever you have to do to find the time to let yourself enjoy a small part of your day. If you keep a daily to-do list, write "My Ten Minutes" on it and think of it as you would any other required task or activity. A friend of mine is an aspiring writer who also has a full-time job and is working on her master's degree. Needless to say, her life is crazy busy, but she often e-mails me a few poems or short stories that she manages to write during her ecstatic moments.

It doesn't matter at all what you choose to do with your ecstatic moments, as long as it's something you absolutely love and enjoy. Juggle, stretch into a yoga pose, write poetry, read a book by your favorite author, work on the birdhouse you've designed, plant your garden, make jewelry, go for a long walk or run or swim or bike ride—anything, as long as it makes you ecstatic! This is your ten minutes to spend doing what you love to do instead of what you should or must or really have to. Use these minutes well and one day you might find yourself spending much more than ten minutes a day doing something that makes you really happy. The idea to write this book you're reading was born during my daily minutes spent with my Book Ideas Journal and countless hours later I can cross an item off my Life Wish List and call myself an author.

DARING FEMALE IDEAS FOR ECSTATIC MOMENTS

- Read your favorite book.
- Paint—walls or paintings.
- Call your best friend.
- Go for a long walk.
- Stand on your head.
- Practice your piano/guitar/violin.
- Dance around your house.
- Make handmade cards.
- Go to a museum.
- Sing along to your favorite CD.
- Watch a part of your all-time favorite movie.
- Organize your life.
- Make funky jewelry.

- Cook up your favorite recipe.
- Work on your scrapbook.
- Play silly with your kids.
- Go for an exhilarating run.
- Work on your novel.
- Read the Sunday paper from cover to cover.
- Write a letter to a friend.
- Meditate.
- Take a bubble bath.
- Spend a moment in silence.
- Spend time with someone you love.
- Redecorate your house.
- Sip a perfect latte.

TAKE ON THE DARE

Write down a few things that make you ecstatic and dare to spend at least ten minutes each day doing one of them.

_____

_____

_____

_____

_____

_____

Dare to Learn Something New Every Day

DARE-METER

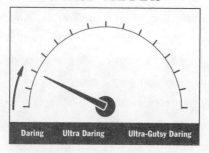

The excitement of learning separates you from old age. As long as you're learning, you're not old.

—ROSALYN YALOW, AMERICAN MEDICAL PHYSICIST

For much of our lives, when we're in school or college, the only responsibility we have is to learn. Whether it's solving math problems, reading history books, writing long essays, or learning to paint, we spend years living a wonderful life of doing little else but gaining knowledge and learning new skills. Then real life happens, and for most of us, every day turns into a series of routines, which often leave too little time and energy for learning new things. Sure, we're learning all the time—through interacting with other people; working; reading newspapers, magazines, and books; watching TV; and just soaking in what happens in the world around us. But when was the last time that you learned something completely new and unfamiliar, something you were interested in or curious about?

Dare yourself to learn something new every day! Learning new skills and ideas keeps us alive, energized, and growing, making life much more fun and interesting. Beyond indulging our curiosity, which by itself is a great reason to do it, constant learning offers new opportunities and paths that we might never consider otherwise. You might never think of starting your own business, but then happen to read an article about clothing trends among teens and get an idea to design your own clothing line. Or you might sign up for a cooking class to learn how to make more than toast and pasta, fall in love with cooking, and go on to become a chef. You never know where life will take you, but the more you learn, the greater the number of opportunities that you open up for yourself.

Countless studies show that keeping our brains working and learning new skills keeps us younger, staving off disease. I recently read an article about a study published in *The New England Journal of Medicine* demonstrating that engaging in mind-stimulating activities—everything from learning a foreign language to reading poetry—helped prevent or minimize the memory loss often associated with getting older. To me, this is just a nice bonus. Every time you learn something, you rejuvenate yourself and add another dimension to your life. And that's the most wonderful and honest reason to dare yourself to always be learning something new. Don't worry about how what you learn fits into your life: Making pottery might be an unlikely hobby for an investment banker, but I think it makes you a pretty cool investment banker. If something interests you, learn about it, invest some time in it, and color your life with what you learn from it. It's impossible to predict how the things you learn might affect your life, and the surprises are a big part of the enjoyment of learning.

A few years ago I decided to try my hand at painting. While living in Japan during college I became addicted to a type of Japanese ink painting called Sumi-e. This time I wanted to try something different, but I didn't have time for a class, so I went to an art store and decided to just browse around. There was a sale on gel and acrylic paints; I took that as a sign to try my hand at abstract painting. I bought some supplies and on the way home looked for something to paint. I live in New York City, where inspiration is not hard to find. A street vendor a few blocks from my apartment was selling huge canvases he had painted with funky patterns. He used watercolor, but seeing them gave me an idea to try the same style of painting in 3-D, using my newly acquired gels. I came home and got to work. Two dozen attempts later I finally figured out how to make gel stick to paper without running down to the floor. To my surprise I actually liked some of the funky canvases I painted. I'm no Picasso, but that day I found one of the most relaxing pastimes I've ever experienced.

Something that's really fun to do once a year is to write down everything you've learned. (You can do this on your birthday or around New Year's.) Grab your journal or a notebook and write down everything you've picked up that year: new things you can do, interesting ideas you discovered, memorable facts you've read about, new qualities you found in yourself or people around you. Thinking over what you've learned can be extremely empowering and make you realize you're always growing and changing.

Life is short, most of us don't have a lot of free time, and there is always more to do on our lists than we can handle. But finding a few minutes each day to learn something is like eating or sleeping or breathing. If you want to truly LIVE, you've got to do it. And remember that learning is not just an occasional activity but a way of life, a Daring Female attitude that keeps your eyes, ears, brain, and heart open to as many new experiences and ideas as possible.

DARING FEMALE IDEAS FOR LEARNING

- Read one magazine or newspaper article every day from sections that you usually skip.
- Sign up for a class—in person or online—in something outside of what you do every day, like writing, glassblowing, Spanish guitar, cooking, or tap dancing.
- Learn a skill you've always wished you had, like speaking another language or being able to draw.
- Read a book on a subject you know very little about—how about politics, feng shui, photography, or the history of duct tape?
- Sign up for a daily learning e-mail. For example, check out www.wordsmith.org, where you can sign up to get a daily e-mail with a new word and its definition.
- Buy a trivia page-a-day calendar and take a minute to read it every day.
- Ask a friend to take you along to her knitting/creative writing/weird movie lovers/painting group.
- Buy a funky cookbook and whip up recipes you've never tried to cook before.
- Take a different way home and check out new and unfamiliar places along the way.

TAKE ON THE DARE

Take a few minutes right now and write down a few things/ideas/skills that you'd like to learn, but more important, dare to pick one and start learning it right away!

_____

_____

_____

_____

_____

_____

Dare to Do Now What You Could Do Later

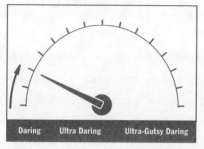

DARE-METER

Daring   Ultra Daring   Ultra-Gutsy Daring

Delay breeds fear.

—JESSAMYN WEST, AMERICAN NOVELIST

How many times have you looked at something on your to-do list, especially if it's something you aren't too thrilled about doing in the first place, and thought, "Ah, I'll get to this later"? I bet we are all guilty of this more often than we think, arming ourselves with great excuses like being too tired, too busy, or too focused on something else. But however great the excuse, it doesn't accomplish the most important thing: get the task off the to-do list. And as long as it's there, whether written down or simply on your mind, it's a burden, an annoyance, and something that sucks up energy you could be using to do things that you actually enjoy.

Dare to do now what you could do later! Be a bulldog when it comes to your to-do list; attack it like there's nothing else in sight. As you get things done, you'll feel productive and in control of your life. You'll clear your mind and be able to think about more important and fun things than cleaning out your closets or scheduling a dentist appointment (at which you know you'll have to hear a long and unpleasant lecture about taking better care of your teeth). Make a commitment to yourself that if you can find a way to do something now, regardless of how easy the task is to put off until tomorrow or next week or next month, you'll take care of it and move on with your life.

Sometimes, of course, you might really have to delay doing something until later because your to-do list is so long that not even a superhuman Daring Female could get everything done. This is when it gets really ugly, and after having had too many unpleasant days like this, I now try to practice restraint when deciding what goes on my to-do list. I like to write things down, so every morning before I drink my coffee or turn on my computer, I jot down my work-related and personal to-dos for the day. As I do, I think about when I'll have time to do each task, and if I can't envision getting it done, I leave it off the list. I love crossing items off my to-do list; I feel this great sense of accomplishment and satisfaction when I do it. On the flip side, if I get to only half of my to-dos I feel unproductive and overwhelmed, two emotions that every Daring Female should fight with all her power. There are still too many times when I have things left undone, but I'm getting better about judging my time and realizing that most days are still stubborn about being only twenty-four hours long.

You might be wondering why this is such big deal; hey, if you can do something later, no harm done. And when we're talking about scheduling a dentist appointment, as long as you don't put if off for years, that's probably okay. But I find that how we deal with things on a day-to-day basis is often very similar to the way we live our lives: If you put off the small stuff on your daily to-do list, you might well be putting off some big stuff on your life to-do list. Getting into great shape, moving to a city where you've always wanted to live, beginning to write the next great American novel, changing your career path—putting off life changes as big as these has a much greater impact on your life than failing to pick up your dry cleaning on time. Of course, sometimes you have to delay doing one thing in your life because you're pursuing another goal. If you've just bought a house for which you've been saving up for years and need a secure source of income, then a new career adventure will probably have to wait. But if you're delaying making big life decisions because you're scared or averse to risk, or because you think there will be an ideal time for it later on, you might be missing out on making your life as rewarding as it could be.

There rarely is an ideal time to make a big life change

and life has an awful way of rushing by us far faster than we realize. You've got to remember what's on your life to-do list and always look for an opportunity to accomplish something and cross it off. If you decide to wait and not make a change today, how do you know that you'll make it tomorrow or a year from now?

Dare to do now what you could do later. For example, if you don't like your job, start doing something about it. Begin to think about changing jobs and start checking out other opportunities in your field. Or consider staying where you are but changing your responsibilities; put together a proposal to discuss with your boss. Go to the bookstore and buy a career advice book or call up an old mentor for advice. Whatever you do, don't wait and hope that things will change on their own or that somehow in a month you'll be in a better place in your life to do something about it. Do something now, take a concrete action, and feel like a powerful and productive Daring Female in control of your life. Of course, there's no guarantee that every step you take will lead you in the right direction, but there's huge value in knowing that you're not standing still.

DARING FEMALE "DO THIS NOW EVEN IF YOU CAN DO IT LATER" IDEAS

- Schedule an appointment you've been putting off.
- Redecorate a room in your house that you can't stand.
- Get into great shape.
- Figure out what you really want to do with your life and start doing it.
- Change jobs.
- Ask for a promotion or a raise.
- Ask out that guy with whom you've been flirting for the past year.
- End a going-nowhere relationship.
- Take your dream vacation.
- Start working on the next great American novel.
- Create a plan for starting your dream business.
- Figure out your finances and come up with a financial plan for the future.

TAKE ON THE DARE

Write down a few to-dos that you've been putting off for a while, and starting this week, dare to tackle at least one.

_____

_____

_____

_____

_____

_____

Dare to Look Forward More Often Than You Look Back

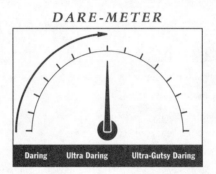

DARE-METER

Daring   Ultra Daring   Ultra-Gutsy Daring

Mistakes are part of the dues one pays for a full life.
—SOPHIA LOREN, ITALIAN ACTRESS

Several years ago I quit a secure, well-paying job with a prestigious consulting firm to work for a small start-up with an uncertain future. My desire to get my hands dirty and help a small team run a company was too strong to resist. Without much research or pondering over my risky decision, I made the jump.

This particular story does not have a rosy ending. I did not learn a lot or make lots of money or find a lifelong mentor. The company I joined turned out to be extremely dysfunctional and popped the dot-com bubble just a few months after my first day. Less than a year after I made the jump to the start-up world I had to leave.

I was devastated, and not just because I was out of a job in a tough job market or because leaving my earlier job at the consulting firm just two months before my two-year anniversary meant I'd given up a great number of perks and benefits. I was devastated mostly because, looking back, I felt I'd made my decision to switch jobs too quickly, without giving it much thought. I felt really stupid and kept beating myself up for letting my impulsiveness take over.

Eventually I got a job that put me on a more creative and interesting career path. I also stopped wallowing in self-pity and regret. I had to be honest about my mistake to make sure I didn't make it again. I can't ever *not* be impulsive—that's a big part of the wacky crazy Daring Female that I am—but now I have a rule that I try to stick to whenever I'm about to make a big life change. It's simple, but it works: I impose a waiting period on myself. This means that I'm not allowed to make any decisions for one week, even if I'm absolutely positively certain that I know what I want to do. I don't sit around rethinking my decision or second-guessing myself. My waiting period is more of a chance to catch my breath and make sure that I still have a good gut feeling about making a change. If at the end of the week I still do, then I go ahead and never look back. And while a week might not seem long to you, trust me, for an impulsive jump-into-things person like me, it's close to forever.

Dare to look forward more often than you look back! We all make mistakes and we all regret making them. It's human and a part of life. But I've found that when we realize we've made the wrong choice or decision, it becomes too easy for us to get lost in thoughts of the "woulda/coulda/shoulda" variety. This is fine for a short while until you get these feelings out of your system, but continuing to regret things you've done in your life is unproductive and can make you more miserable than you need to be. So while you can't avoid regrets altogether, you can turn them into lessons to help you make better choices in the future.

Try this: The next time you realize that you've made a mistake or taken a wrong turn, and your head begins to fill with "woulda/coulda/shoulda" thoughts, take out a piece of paper and write some of them down in a column. Then use the Daring Female Rearview Mirror Transformer and change each one into a practical tip you can use in the future to avoid making the same mistake. Say, for example, that you lose your cool with your husband/boyfriend/partner for being late before you find out that he had one of those rare good reasons to be late (and they are extremely rare!). Your head fills up with a bunch of "woulda/coulda/shoulda" thoughts, which probably run something like "I should've let him explain why he didn't show up on time instead of launching into a tirade." Here's a perfect opportunity to use your Daring Female power to transform these thoughts into something more productive, like "The next time I get angry at someone I am going to give him a chance to explain his actions before I start yelling." And after you've changed your regrets into an action plan for the future, take some time and let it soak into your system. You've got to make sure that the next time a similar situation comes up, you will act in a way that won't lead to "woulda/coulda/shoulda" land.

One Daring Female who lives the anti-"woulda/coulda/ shoulda" mantra is Betty Deitch. I learned about Betty while doing research for this book. During the infamous dot-com boom and bust, Betty and her husband lost a great deal of money in the stock market. I'm sure they were extremely upset and angry at both themselves and the market for making such a dent in their finances. And I'm sure that the easiest thing for Betty to do was to get lost in regrets about investing the money in the first place, not getting it out at the right time, not hiring the right broker, not firing the wrong broker soon enough, and so on. But instead, Betty and her husband invented, designed, and began to market a board game called the Wall Street Spin, an entertaining game that lets people try their hand at playing the stock market without taking any risks. In creating the game, Betty hoped that it would lift the spirits of many of us who've lost a dollar or a fortune in the stock market.

I think that's a pretty awesome way to take on the dare to look forward more often than you look back. I dare you to do the same in your life the next opportunity you get. Today seems like the perfect time to start, don't you think?

DARING FEMALE REARVIEW MIRROR TRANSFORMER

"WOULDA/COULDA/SHOULDA"	"WILL/CAN/SHALL"
I should've asked my boss how to structure my presentation instead of swinging it without any guidance.	In the future I'm not going to be afraid to ask for help and will see it as a sign of my professionalism instead of weakness.
I could've gotten credit for how well the project turned out if I had spoken up at the meeting instead of staying quiet the entire time.	In the future I'm going to speak up when I have something to say instead of being afraid to stand out.
If I'd been more honest about what I liked to do for fun instead of trying to say what I thought he wanted to hear, we might have hit it off.	In the future I'm going to be honest and be myself instead of trying to please other people by saying what I think they want to hear.
I shouldn't have eaten that extra piece of cake and given up the healthy way in which I'd been eating for the past few months.	In the future I'm not going to let one slipup ruin my efforts to stay healthy. I'll just forget about it and get back to my healthy routine.

TAKE ON THE DARE

Write down a few regrets that hound you. Then stop dwelling on the past and dare to transform each one into a useful lesson for the future, using the Rearview Mirror Transformer.

_____

_____

_____

_____

_____

_____

Dare to Stop Frustration with Action

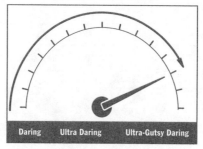

DARE-METER

Daring   Ultra Daring   Ultra-Gutsy Daring

It's better to wear out than to rust out.

—FRANCES WILLARD,
AMERICAN EDUCATOR AND REFORMER

I don't know why, but I find feeling frustrated extremely draining and tiring. Whether the frustration has to do with my job, my family, or my writing, I find it unbearable, and at the first sign of it, I run from it as fast as I can. Well, I don't literally start running (although some might find this helpful), but I do put my anti-frustration battle plan into action. And what is my anti-frustration battle plan? It's so simple you might laugh: At the first sign of frustration I stop and immediately do something to change whatever is making me feel frustrated. Say I look in the mirror and it fails to hide the effects of the last few months, when I forgot (or was too lazy) to make time for exercise. As I feel frustration wash over me, I turn away from the mirror, and unless there is absolutely no way for me to do it, I get my heart pumping. If I'm home, I run to the gym. If I'm at work, I go walking for twenty minutes. If I can't get away that very moment, getting some exercise is the first thing I do when I find a free minute.

The most important part of my less-than-sophisticated anti-frustration battle plan is to take action, to do something concrete and specific, and to do it as soon as I begin to feel frustrated. I've heard advice about taking a break from whatever is frustrating you and coming back to it later, but this doesn't work for me. Just walking away from the mirror when I don't like what I see solves nothing. The less-than-pleasant image of myself I just saw will stick in my head, and as I dwell on it, will make me feel worse. But when I do something about it, regardless of the obvious fact that just that one action—going to the gym or for a quick walk—won't magically make everything perfect, I feel in control of my feelings instead of letting them control me. If I'm smart about the first step, it helps me continue to take actions that deal with my frustration (when I go to the gym, I feel good, which is a great incentive to go again).

Dare to stop frustration with action! Whatever technique you've been using until now—like climbing into your bed and hiding under the covers or eating a box of chocolate chip cookies—give it a break and try this one. The next time you start to feel frustrated, stop what you're doing, think about it, and immediately take an action that puts you in control of your frustration and does something to counter it. Here are a few ideas, in case you need some inspiration:

Frustration	Ideas for Immediate Action
You're stumped by a project at work and after many late nights and cups of coffee still can't figure out how to approach it.	Invite a smart-cookie colleague out to lunch and ask for her input.
	If you're having problems figuring out how to approach the project, choose one small part of it and work on that piece instead (and don't think about how it will work with the rest of what you have to do, at least for now).
You've been trying to explain to your husband/boyfriend/significant other how you feel about a certain issue and you seem to get nowhere.	Change the setting: Go for a walk to talk about it, meet in person if you've been talking on the phone, consider writing down how you feel and giving the note to your partner.
	Do something creative, such as playing your own version of Pictionary, where you draw, instead of trying to verbally explain, how you feel and why.

Frustration	Ideas for Immediate Action
You've been diligently saving money to buy a new house or go on an exotic vacation, but you just don't seem to be able to save enough.	Call up a financial adviser (ask for recommendations from friends and family) and schedule a meeting to go over your finances.
	Sit down with a calculator and a clean sheet of paper (or use a spreadsheet program, if you're a computer whiz) and estimate how much money you'll need. Be realistic and frugal. You might realize that you don't need quite as much as you thought.
You've been trying to get into great shape for the summer, but the endless trips to the gym don't seem to get you the results you want.	Go to the gym and sign up for a session with a personal trainer. It will cost you, but you may uncover a few things you can add to your workout to make it more effective.
	The next time you go to the gym, change your routine completely. Try different machines, go for a longer or a shorter period of time, and check out an exercise class that looks fun, such as Pilates or Striptease Cardio (I'm not kidding).

Remember, an essential part of being a Daring Female is knowing that you have power to do whatever you want with your life—and unabashedly exercising that power as often as possible. When something in your life starts to make you frustrated (or maybe you've been frustrated about it way too long and want to stop feeling that way), use that power and take action. It might actually help you deal with whatever is frustrating you. Or at the very least, it will make you feel in control of what's going on in your life. And when you feel in control you have a much greater chance of figuring out how to kick your frustrations in the butt. Things change when you change them, so be true to your Daring Female self and change frustration into feelings of accomplishment, inventiveness, and satisfaction.

DARING FEMALE ANTI-FRUSTRATION BATTLE PLAN

The next time you feel frustrated, use this mini-questionnaire to come up with a battle plan to help you feel less so. But never forget the most important step: Dare to put your battle plan into action with the full force of your Daring Female power!

1. What is frustrating me?
2. Why?
3. What have I done about it before?
4. Did it work?
5. What can I do about it right this minute?
6. What can I do about it in the longer term?

TAKE ON THE DARE

Create your own anti-frustration battle plan for whatever is driving you nuts and dare to follow it with full confidence that you can succeed.

_____

_____

_____

_____

_____

_____

Dream
Huge, Aim
Higher

D F If you discover just one Daring Female quality and make it part of your life, let it be the ability to stretch your imagination and dream the wildest dreams. Nothing limits us more than the boundaries we create for ourselves. Don't let the hectic routines of your days prevent you from thinking about the future, making plans, and having dreams. No one else can dream for you and no one else can aim higher than you can. But leave the job of doubting yourself or your ability to realize your dreams to someone else—don't waste an ounce of energy on this. Dream huge, aim high, and believe that everything you imagine *can* happen.

Dare to Have a Life Wish List and Cross Something Off Every Year

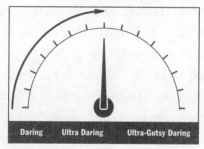

DARE-METER

Daring   Ultra Daring   Ultra-Gutsy Daring

One must desire something to be alive.

—MARGARET DELAND, AMERICAN NOVELIST

A few years ago I was working with a woman named Stephanie. We were both slaving away at a consulting company where eighteen-hour days were the norm, and if you got a weekend off you felt lucky. Time for anything outside of work besides scarce sleep and food was so limited that I began to feel that I lived at my job. And no matter how much you might like your work—and I liked this particular job—doing nothing but work is stifling, and can eventually drive you nuts.

One day I walked into Stephanie's office to see if she wanted to grab some lunch. She wasn't there, so I decided to leave a note on her corkboard. Hanging from her bulletin board was a piece of paper, at the top of which the words "One Day I Wish To" were written. I decided to snoop and kept reading, soon realizing that I'd stumbled upon Stephanie's Life Wish List. "Scuba dive, read a book in one sitting, visit every continent, work less" were some of the entries on her list. This was her escape from the endless projects and clients and meetings, a way for her to remember what she wanted from her life.

Until I saw Stephanie's Life Wish List I was the victim of making a long list of unrealistic New Year's resolutions every year. (Losing twenty pounds by spring sound familiar to anyone?) I realized that keeping a Life Wish List was a much better idea, so I came home that day and started mine. I pulled a new journal from my stationery stash—you've got to have one of those—and wrote down things I wanted to do, experience, and achieve in my life. Here are some things I put on my Life Wish List:

- Become a published author.
- Learn how to swim properly.
- Spend a week in Paris at least once every two years.
- Learn how to downhill ski.
- Have a painting studio in my house and take painting lessons.
- Run my own company without giving up everything else in my life.

I visit my Life Wish List often (although never during New Year's celebrations), rewrite and add to it, and try to make sure that I cross something off every year. It's a great reminder of what I'm after in life and a reflection of how I change every year. (What was I thinking when I put bungee jumping on my list?) The time I spend with my Life Wish List is always a great way to escape from a bad day or a sad mood.

Dare to have a Life Wish List and cross something off every year! Get away from the insanity of your day-to-day life and think about what you want to do and experience before . . . well, you know. Dream huge and don't edit your thoughts. It doesn't matter how wacky or improbable your life wishes seem, write them down. No one is going to grade you on your Life Wish List. This is your personal space to be honest and daring and gutsy about what you want to get out of your life. And if ten years from now your life wishes seem silly or crazy—well then, you'll get a laugh out of it.

Dare yourself to revisit and rewrite your Life Wish List often and use it to push yourself to get as much as you can out of your life, making sure that you get what you love and want and care about. If something on your list seems difficult to achieve but you care about it, try your hardest to find a way to make it happen. Remember, you don't have to do it today, next month, or even next year. This wish list is for your life, and if you commit to making something happen, who cares how long it takes!

One of the things I find most challenging about my Life

Wish List is not to feel like a complete loser when I can't cross off more than a few things after a long period of time. Sometimes I fall into the trap of thinking of this as my to-do list. But then I remind myself that a Life Wish List is completely different: It has no immediate deadline, and it can change as often as I do. Some things you wrote down a year ago might not seem that important now, while you've added some new goals. And remember, if you've accomplished only a few things on your Life Wish List, it might be a lot more than you would've done if you hadn't created the list in the first place. Think of it as a lifelong journal of wishes, dreams, and goals, and use it as your inspiration rather than as something to stress about.

DARING FEMALE LIFE WISH LIST IDEAS

- Places you'd like to visit
- People you'd like to meet
- Ideas you want to explore
- Feelings you want to experience
- Skills you want to learn
- Habits you want to kick
- Habits you want to have

- Adventures you'd like to experience
- Jobs you'd like to have
- Businesses you want to start
- Books you want to write
- Books you want to read
- Movies you want to make
- Ways you want to change the world

TAKE ON THE DARE

Start now! Take a few minutes and write down some of your goals and wishes for the next many, many years. I've left some space below for you to get started, but I suggest that you create and keep a separate Life Wish List. Go to your favorite stationery store and find a small, durable journal or notebook. Keep it in your purse or in a special place at home, and read and add to it often. But most important, dare to use your Life Wish List as inspiration to go after what you want, what makes you truly happy.

_____

_____

_____

_____

_____

_____

Dare to Chase Your Passions

DARE-METER

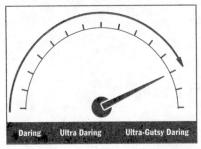

Daring Ultra Daring Ultra-Gutsy Daring

Just don't give up trying to do what you really want to do.
Where there is love and inspiration, I don't think
you can go wrong.

—ELLA FITZGERALD, AMERICAN JAZZ SINGER

I'd never wondered about why we use the word *chase* when we talk about going after what we want and following our passions, but the reason became crystal clear to me shortly after I decided to start a publishing company with my husband. I've always wanted to create something from scratch, something new and innovative. For years I've been writing down ideas for products and businesses in my numerous Idea Journals, hoping that one day I'd have enough time, money, and experience to pursue one of them with full force. Well, one thing I've learned is that there never seems to be a perfect time to pursue your life passions or dreams—you can always argue that you don't have enough time or money or experience. Sometimes you just have to decide to go for it—and we did.

That's when it hit me: This was going to be a long, tough chase, with absolutely no guarantee of success. Neither I nor my husband had any clue about publishing books or running a company, and once we started to get our bearings and do some research, we felt overwhelmed and intimidated. I remember thinking that this might be too much for two people to handle part-time while holding down day jobs, without any experience, and on a tiny budget. In retrospect, it was a pretty crazy idea, but the fire in my belly was like a little engine that kept me going. I really, really wanted this!

We'd go off to our bill-paying day jobs in the morning, come back at night, manage to grab a quick bite, and then start our second jobs as newly minted publishers. Our weekends quickly turned into full working days and we spent less time with friends, going out, and just doing the simple things we enjoyed, such as hanging out on a Saturday afternoon and reading the paper.

I knew that trying to get a company off the ground while working full-time was going to be hard, but I never imagined that it was going to be as hard as it turned out to be or that we'd have to give up so much. I'd look outside on a beautiful spring Sunday afternoon, while we were working in our apartment, and every fiber in my body would want to give it all up and just run out and spend the day relaxing in the park. I'd feel this powerful nostalgia for days when we didn't have to worry about printer delays, writer temper tantrums, and endless bills that were quickly wiping out our savings. Some days I felt close to breaking down under all the pressure and lack of sleep. Somehow I kept going, not the least because my husband was an incredible support and my auxiliary energy source, and someone who kept reminding me that this was something I'd wanted for as long as he knew me.

After two years of the most difficult chase I'd ever undertaken we did have our publishing company: Our books were on shelves in stores and in the hands of some happy customers. I remember the exhilaration that overwhelmed me the first time we went to Barnes & Noble and saw our books—I literally felt on top of the world. I realized that I felt this way for two reasons: I'd made one of my life dreams come true and I had worked so crazy hard to do it. And I couldn't tell you which of the two reasons made me happier or prouder. All I know is that now I had an arsenal of confidence and endurance for the next time I decided to attempt one of my crazy feats!

Dare to chase your passions! It may not be easy—actually, I can almost guarantee you that it won't be and most likely it will be a long race rather than a quick sprint. The pursuit will involve obstacles, doubts, exhaustion, unpleasant surprises, and many other things you won't be able to foresee before you start. And you should take it on only if you can truly say a resounding yes to all of the following:

- This is truly my passion, something I love and want to be part of my life.
- I understand that I will have to commit to chasing my passion for a long time, probably longer than I think it should take.
- I am willing to work really hard, probably harder than I've ever worked in my life.
- I will enjoy the actual chase, as well as the final outcome, even though the path toward my goal will be difficult and on some days I'll probably want to quit and not work so hard.

Tama Kieves waited many years before leaving her secure job as a Harvard-educated corporate lawyer to indulge her true passion for writing to start on her first book. And she took another twelve years to write it. For most of those years, Tama's toughest job was overcoming her self-doubts: She worried that she wouldn't be able to get the book published, that she wasn't writing it fast enough, that there were ten thousand competitive books on the market. Every time she saw a similar book hit the shelves she wanted to throw in the towel and give it all up. But becoming an author was something that she had wanted to do since high school, when she'd read *Catcher in the Rye* and fallen in love with books and writing. Each time Tama felt that she wanted to give up chasing her passion she dug deep, remembered why it was so important to her, and kicked her efforts into a higher gear. Her book, *This Time I Dance! Trusting the Journey of Creating the Work You Love*, was eventually published by J. P. Tarcher, and she went on to found a successful personal coaching business based on the advice in the book. (You can check it out on Tama's Web site, www.awakeningartistry.com.) By daring herself to follow her passion, Tama created a life she was always after. Imagine how awesome that must have felt!

Whatever your passion may be—writing a book, becoming a singer, designing a house, making the world a cleaner place to live—you have to be mentally and physically prepared for the chase. I've never been a runner, but I imagine this process is somewhat like preparing for a marathon and then committing yourself to finishing it, even though you may be gasping for air, feeling your muscles contract with pain, and wondering what in the world possessed you to do this. You will make it to the finish line and achieve your goal only if what you're chasing is something you want badly and for which you're willing to work incredibly hard.

I use this simple trick when I am chasing a goal: I create a short list of reasons for why I am doing it and keep it where I can see it, in my planner or taped to my computer screen. Having this constant reminder in front of me is surprisingly powerful, and I suggest that you try this the next time you're out there chasing your passion. Come up with five reasons that show you care about what you're doing and use the list as your personal cheerleader at times when you feel like giving up. I think this is also a great test of how badly you want to go after each particular goal. If you can't come up with five great reasons to prove you want something, then maybe you need to rethink whether you want to chase it after all. Life is short and you want to spend it going after things you genuinely care about.

DARING FEMALE TOOL KIT FOR CHASING YOUR PASSIONS

Don't start your chase without this tool kit, filled with the essential ingredients you'll need to succeed.

- Obsessive desire to get what you're after

- Confidence in your ability to succeed and to enjoy the process (even if you don't)

- Commitment to keep going when you are most certain that you can't

- Endless energy

- Willingness to have less time for other parts of your life—sleep, relaxation, fun—for as long as it takes

- Full reserve of self-pep talk (don't forget to use your Daring Female Rearview Mirror Transformer)

- A source of support and encouragement: your partner, your family, your friends, reminders about other people who've done what you're attempting

- An in-your-face reminder of why you're chasing your passion, such as a mantra you write out and paste in your daily planner, on your fridge, or on your computer screen

TAKE ON THE DARE

Write down two of your strongest passions. Dare to create a plan and start chasing one of them, regardless of how daunting or improbable the chase might seem.

_____

_____

_____

_____

_____

_____

Dare to Bite Off More Than You Can Chew, but Learn How to Spit

DARE-METER

Daring   Ultra Daring   Ultra-Gutsy Daring

Learning too soon our limitations, we never learn our powers.

—MIGNON MCLAUGHLIN, AMERICAN HUMORIST

All right, here's a challenge for you: The next time you're faced with a task, a challenge, or many tasks and challenges all at once, and you think, "Wow, there's no way I can do this," stop. Slam on the brakes in your head and turn your thoughts around until you think, "Okay, this is tough, but I can handle it." It might feel like you're trying to turn a car on an icy road and you may not get it right on the first attempt (or the first ten), but be stubborn and tough and get there, at least in your mind. And if you can't make yourself genuinely believe that you can do something, fake it. No, this is not a typo. Sometimes we need to pretend that we can take on more than seems possible before we actually believe that we can. So go ahead, pretend a little.

Believing that you can take on the world is step one, of course. Step two is taking on the world. And I honestly can't tell you which one is more difficult. A few years ago I was offered a great position with a small technology company—good news in a bad job climate. The scary news was that the job involved much more responsibility than I'd ever handled, I had relatively little experience in the industry, and there was no formal training involved. If I took this on, I'd have to figure it all out on my own and do it really, really fast. Although I had no other job prospects at the time, I did consider turning down this job offer. What if I couldn't figure it out? What if once I joined the bigwigs, they realized that they made a mistake? What if I had to work twenty-nine hours a day to get the job done and never saw sunlight again? A few weeks and many more thoughts like this later, I made up my mind to take the job. I decided that if the guys who offered me the position thought I could do it, I should think so, too. And as much as I thought I knew what I was in for, I had absolutely no idea how insane a challenge it would be. I considered quitting oh, maybe ten times on a good day and a hundred times on a bad one, and I spent many weeks working more than I'd ever wanted or thought I could. It was crazy, intimidating, and difficult, but I managed to get the hang of it after a while (and felt pretty proud of myself for doing it).

Dare to bite off more than you can chew. Take on more than you think you can handle, go for a goal you think is not reachable, do stuff that you would usually consider out of your reach, and prove to yourself that you're capable of more than you think. More often than not we're limited by our own imagination and perception of our abilities: If you think you can't do something, you won't attempt it. Well, throw that thought out the window and dare yourself to take on the world:

- Apply for that job that seems out of your reach instead of sticking to jobs you know you can handle.
- Take an advanced class in something you've always wanted to learn.
- Get into the greatest shape of your life instead of just good shape.
- Take a leadership position on a tough project at work even if you don't know exactly how you'll handle it.
- Train for a marathon instead of a 10K.

What's the worst that can happen? You stretch your imagination and take on more than you can handle and find yourself not being able to do it. You're out of breath, exhausted, and cranky. Or your body is aching and hurting from the crazy marathon routine you're putting it through. Instead of feeling like a powerful Daring Female you're tired and unhappy and realize that you really *did* bite off more than you can chew. What do you do then?

First, let me save you the suspense: If you dare yourself

to stretch your limits and reach high in life, there will most definitely come a time when you realize that you've reached too high. And when you do bite off more than you can chew, you have to learn how to spit. You have to slow down or give up something altogether, and you have to get back to feeling great and upbeat rather than exhausted and cranky. It's not easy to decide whether the difficulty you're encountering is something you should work through on your way to your goal or a sign that you need to reconsider and perhaps slow down. I don't think that any worthwhile achievement comes without loads of sweat, tremendous effort, and many days when you feel two minutes away from quitting. But there is a difference, however subtle at times, between feeling invigorated by a challenge, albeit exhausted at times on your way to meeting it, and feeling mentally and physically worn out all the time.

So how can you tell the difference? I suggest taking a break from whatever you're doing. If you've been training for a marathon, take a few days off; if you've been taking a night class, skip a few. If after a short break you feel the urge to get back to your challenge and find yourself filled with new energy to do it, then I say go for it. On the flip side, if you find that you're dreading getting back to what you were doing and feel much happier without it, then consider the idea that perhaps you bit off more than you could chew.

I have a wonderful friend who is a Daring Female if ever there was one. She's full of energy and ideas, and lives every moment of her life as if it were the only moment she'll ever have. A few months ago she decided to take night classes to become a court reporter. She commutes two hours to work each day and wanted to gain a skill that eventually would let her work closer to home. So two times a week she'd run from her day job to her three-hour class, and then hop on a bus for the long ride home. I watched her get increasingly more tired every week, but she kept at it for the full semester, until she had a chance to take a breather and realized that perhaps she had taken on more than she could deal with. She was exhausted, had given up doing other things that made her happy, and found herself without any mental energy to live her life. She didn't want to feel like a quitter and struggled with what to do. Eventually she realized that this just wasn't the right time to add yet another activity to her already overcrowded schedule. She put off taking the next level of the class until she could free up more time. She told me that she was sad to quit but knew it was the right thing at that moment.

Dare to bite off more than you can chew, but learn how to spit! You're not a failure or a quitter if you attempt a challenge but find that you can't tackle it while keeping your sanity. You're an honest, realistic, and awesome Daring Female who takes on the world and knows when to slow down and when to try it again. This is a much better way to live then shying away from opportunities or tasks that seem too difficult. After all, if you *never* feel like you're doing too much, then how do you know that you're getting everything you possibly can out of your life?

DARING FEMALE IMAGINATION STRETCHER

YOU MIGHT THINK . . .	DARING FEMALE THINKS . . .
This is way over my head.	This is way over my head, but I'm going to give it a shot.
I don't think I can fit one more thing into my insanely busy life.	I can fit this into my life if I get organized and prioritize.
I've never done something like this before, so I shouldn't try it.	I've never done something like this before and I can't wait to try it.
Everyone else seems to think I can do this, but I know I can't.	Everyone else seems to think I can do this, so why shouldn't I think I can?
If I take this on and can't succeed, I'll feel like a complete failure.	If I take this on and can't succeed, I'll know that I had the guts to try and can try again later.
If I take this on and can't succeed, everyone else will think I am a failure.	If I take this on and can't succeed, I'll feel like a gutsy Daring Female and not care about what everyone thinks.

TAKE ON THE DARE

Jot down a few tasks, adventures, or challenges that you've thought about tackling but haven't because they seemed too difficult, too over your head, or too much to handle. Then pick one, dare yourself to do it, and go for it. If it turns out that you really did bite off more than you can chew, use your spitting skills and feel like a Daring Female who always reaches high but who is human and may sometimes need to slow down before tackling another challenge.

_____

_____

_____

_____

_____

_____

Dare to Imitate People Who Inspire You

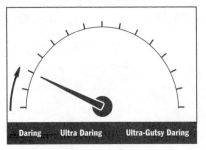

DARE-METER

Daring   Ultra Daring   Ultra-Gutsy Daring

*The most beautiful thing in the world is, precisely, the
conjunction of learning and inspiration.*

—WANDA LANDOWSKA, POLISH PIANIST

One of the greatest sources of inspiration for doing awesome, risky, outrageous, gutsy, unique, creative—in
other words, truly Daring Female—things in your life
is people who have and are doing awesome, risky, outrageous, gutsy, unique, and creative things. They are entrepre-
neurs, writers, moviemakers, artists, performers, inventors,
designers, and everyone in between. Often you don't have to
look hard to find out how they got where they are, what they
have achieved, and what obstacles they have overcome. Their

stories are everywhere—on television, in books and magazines. Often some of the most inspiring people in your life are your family members or friends.

Knowing that someone has done what you dream of doing, that someone has beaten the odds and succeeded is inspiring. It makes challenges seem more surmountable, risks less risky, and disappointments along the way less likely to slow you down. There was a time a few years ago when I felt stuck in a rut: My life was filled with work, errands, and more work, and I couldn't find any time for my creative projects. I needed to believe that one day I could actually make a living out of my creative pursuits, so I started to learn about people who had.

One of the people I came across was H. Jackson Brown, Jr. You might not know his name, but I bet you've seen his books: He created the wonderful *Life's Little Instruction Book*, which spent years on the *New York Times's* bestseller list and has sold millions. He practically invented the category of small inspirational gift books which now occupy shelf upon shelf in bookstores. I really liked his books and was inspired by his life path: It wasn't until later in his life, after he'd worked in advertising for years, that he became an author and made his living that way. On a whim, I decided to write him a letter, telling him about my writing and my dream to one day become a published author. To my huge surprise, he wrote back after a few weeks. We spoke on the phone, and I was so pumped after talking to him, I couldn't sit still. After several months of e-mails, I flew down to Nashville to meet Mr. Brown in person. We spent many hours talking about our lives and ideas, about how he gained his success by being honest in his writing and caring about what he wrote. I can honestly say that it was one of the most memorable and inspiring days in my life, and one which will encourage me to pursue my creative ideas for a long time to come.

Dare to imitate people who inspire you! Seek out people who are doing or have successfully accomplished something you want to and learn as much as possible about their path to success and where they went for their own inspiration and support. Keeping a list of the qualities they have and the specific things they've done can help you figure out how to make your own dreams a reality. You may also find it useful to include things that didn't work; someone else's mistakes could save you a wrong turn or two. Of course, no two paths to success are the same, but the more you find out about people who've done what you'd like to do, the more you'll be able to notice certain characteristics, attitudes, and steps that you can follow in your own quest. There's nothing like experiencing something firsthand and learning from it, but when you're attempting something for the first time you've got to do a little borrowing: You've got to learn from the experiences of other people.

I once took a screenwriting class with Georgia, a woman who wanted to become a film director. As part of a directing class she took one summer, she had an opportunity to make a short film. She was inspired by a famous movie director and many of his influences showed up in the final film. After it was done, she sent a copy to him, with a note saying that she had always admired his work. This big-time director was so impressed with Georgia's film that he invited her to meet him on the set of his next movie, which she did, of course. A year later, she was in Italy, working as an apprentice to this director on the set of his next movie. Talk about inspiration. (I recently reconnected with Georgia and found out that she has just finished and released her first feature film. Wow! To learn more about it, visit www.bdcfilms.com)

Do you dream of one day running your own spa business? Learn about Marcia Kilgore, who founded Bliss, now one of the top spas in New York and London, with a few thousand dollars and out of her three-room apartment. Are you wondering if your special formula for kids' applesauce can sell, as it did for Diane Keaton in the movie *Baby Boom*? Check out the story of Julie Aigner-Clark, who created a video to help her own kids learn about art and music, and then launched Baby Einstein, a super-successful company she eventually sold to Disney for more than $20 million. Have you been working on a cookbook that you hope to publish one day? Vicki Lansky's *Feed Me, I'm Yours*, a collection of easy-to-make recipes for kids, sold hundreds of thousands of copies—without ever hitting the desk of a big publisher. Learn about these amazing women and how they made their dreams come true, and dare to imitate their gutsy attitudes. Besides being an amazing source of inspiration and motivation in your quest, learning about creative, gutsy, generous, inventive, and determined people may give you lots of new ideas for how to approach your life.

A FEW INSPIRING DARING FEMALES

* **Kimberly Peirce** was a relatively inexperienced director when she found financial backing for and directed a controversial movie, *Boys Don't Cry*, which won critical acclaim and whose star won an Oscar for her performance.
* **Martina Navratilova** cares little about her age and continues to kick some serious butt on the tennis court at the age of forty-nine, after winning fifty-eight Grand Slam tournaments and setting more records than imaginable in a single career.
* **Helen Thomas** became the first-ever female member of the White House press corps and went on to have a tremendously successful journalistic career.
* **J. K. Rowling** wrote *Harry Potter*, the biggest children's bestseller of all time, on napkins and scrap paper while taking care of her baby as a single mother on welfare.
* **Kate Winslet** has conquered Hollywood without giving up her passion for small-budget independent films or her beautiful non-stick-figure body.
* **Frida Kahlo** became one of the most well-known women artists despite living with excruciating pain for most of her life.
* **Betsey Johnson** created a successful line of funky, whimsical, and colorful clothing by following her own ideas and passion.
* **Nancy Lublin** founded Dress for Success, a national organization that helps thousands of women every year dress professionally and succeed in their job interviews.
* **Madonna**—does she need a description?

TAKE ON THE DARE

Make a list of a few Daring Females who inspire you with their guts, creativity, generosity, funky style, and anything else. Dare yourself to learn as much as you can about them, to imitate their attitudes and to follow the specific steps they took to achieve their dreams.

_____

_____

_____

_____

_____

Dare to Be the Person You Dream of Being

DARE-METER

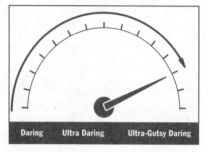

Daring   Ultra Daring   Ultra-Gutsy Daring

> *How we spend our days is, of course,*
> *how we spend our lives.*
> —ANNIE DILLARD, AMERICAN WRITER

Until a few years ago I thought that I had all the time in the world to do what I wanted with my life and to become the kind of person I thought I should be. It felt great to think about all the experience I would gain and what qualities I would develop as time passed. Here's a random selection of characteristics from my Dream Self List, which I created right about the time I started to keep my Life Wish List:

- Be able to let go of long-held preconceptions of myself and gain the freedom to try more new things every day.
- Become more patient and more forgiving of myself and others.
- Spend more days seeing the glass as half full.
- Be a great friend and be surrounded by great friends.
- Have the guts to take risks and the presence of mind not to take dumb risks.
- Judge people less quickly and less harshly.

Then one day it hit me: Life is *now,* not later! I don't have forever to dream about what I want to be in the future. I have to start crossing things off my Dream Self List now, before my life speeds by and turns my dreams into things I should already have learned, become, and done. I don't know what created this new sense of urgency—maybe I realized that each year of my life flew by faster than the one before it—but it was a great kick in the butt! I suddenly felt this huge sense of commitment to do something every day that would bring me closer to being the kind of person I wanted to become.

Dare to be the kind of person you dream of being! All of us have goals and dreams: Some are what we'd like to do and accomplish in life, others are about the kind of person we'd like to be and the qualities for which we'd like to be known. Maybe you want to be more gutsy and ambitious or more patient and balanced. You might dream of being the life of the party or someone on whom friends can always rely for support and an understanding ear. Or maybe you'd like to give up your traditional lifestyle for a more spontaneous one. Whatever it is, don't wait to start doing things or making changes. Do it now! The only way dreams come true is by taking the necessary steps toward them, and making those steps part of our daily routine. There isn't some special period in our lives devoted to realizing our goals (although I do wish there was a national holiday, a Dare to Realize Your Dreams Day when no one would work and we'd focus on our dreams and figuring out how to make them real). The only time we have is right now, and we have to make as much out of now as we possibly can.

So where do you start? I suggest that you take out a piece of paper and write about what kind of person you want to be. You can make it a list of desirable qualities, as I did for my Dream Self List. Or you can write an essay or free-write for a while and see what you come up with. Another possibility is to describe your dream self in the third person. Imagine that your friends are talking about you or your kids (present or future) are describing you to someone else. What would you want them to say? As you work on your Dream Self List, include the qualities you already have and like and those that you want to cultivate. You might be pleasantly surprised to realize that you're living your life close to the way you've described it. Or you might end up describing a person quite different from who you are now. One of the greatest things about being human is that we can and do change. Sure, we come into this world with inborn characteristics, and genes, but we also have the power to choose the way we live out our lives. There's only one catch: It's entirely up to you to use your Daring Female power to get as close as possible to becoming the kind of person that you want to be.

Make sure that you're brutally honest while you are listing the qualities of your dream self. This is your personal list; the only qualities here should be those you care about. Your family doesn't get to weigh in (not even your mother!), and the opinions of your friends and colleagues should not matter either. It's your life—only you get to decide what kind of person you want to be as you're living it. But watch out, because making sure that your Dream Self List is no one's but your own may take more effort than you think. We don't live in isolation and it's easy to be influenced by people, especially those who are close to you. I'm a pretty strong-minded and independent person (some might say too much!) but it took me several tries until I felt that the qualities I put on my list were truly what *I* thought should go on it. For example, one of the qualities I considered was becoming less of a perfectionist, but when I thought carefully about this, I realized that I actually liked being a perfectionist, even though it drives my husband and the rest of my family crazy. Be your own tough editor and make your Dream Self List truly your own!

Of course, just having a Dream Self List doesn't get you very far. You have to do something to make those qualities part of yourself. This is tough. Personally, I can confess that my attempt to become more patient has thus far failed miserably, while my efforts to be less judgmental and more forgiving have paid off. Perhaps patience can never jibe with my impulsive, must-have-it-now personality, but I think my failure so far has more to do with the fact that I haven't done much to teach myself to be more patient. I've ignored my own mantra to follow desires with immediate actions and have simply *wanted* to become more patient. Very non–Daring Female of me and something I must change immediately. In contrast, I can attribute my newly minted more-forgiving personality to a persistent and stubborn effort on my part to not follow my instincts and hold fewer grudges. One of my friends has not called or e-mailed me in months, responding only briefly to my calls and e-mails checking up on her. I was getting upset and felt a major grudge swelling up when I remembered my desire to be more forgiving. So I kept checking up on her and disregarding the fact that I always had to take the initiative. This was completely counterintuitive for me, but it actually made me feel pretty good. What's the point of holding a grudge anyway? I still have to fight my natural inclination to be less forgiving than I'd like to be, but it's becoming easier to do it and I'm becoming more of the kind of person I want to be.

Keep your Dream Self List as a reminder and make every effort possible to behave in ways that get you closer to making those qualities part of who you are. If you'd like to be gutsier, start doing things that are gutsy—speak up, wear an outfit that's so not you, ask for what you want and be specific about how you want it, try something new and unexpected. The key is to actually take concrete steps toward becoming the kind of person you want to be. There must be many ways in which you can practice each quality you'd like to gain. Pick one and start right away.

And here's a kicker: Expect to fail sometimes. If you include items on your list that involve changing something about yourself, it may take a long time and many attempts to succeed. Know this, but view every opportunity as a fresh start, regardless of how you handled it the hundred times before. Like everything else in life, the more you do it, the better at it you'll become: The hundredth time you act in a truly gutsy Daring Female way you might not even realize that you're being gutsy; you'll just think that you're being you!

DARING FEMALE HIGHLY DESIRED QUALITIES

- Expresses herself in every way possible and worries little about anyone's perceptions
- Eager to try and experience new things, making her life sparkle with unanticipated experiences
- Has ambitions and dreams and a strong commitment to taking concrete steps to make them a reality
- Not afraid to share her laughter and positive vibes with the world
- Knows that she doesn't have to conquer the world on her own, but always stays true to her guts and instincts
- Forgets norms, customs, and conventions and struts along her very own path
- Knows what she wants and has the guts to try to make it happen, even if it takes more effort and time than she ever imagined it could
- Doesn't dwell on the past but uses past experiences to guide her in successfully tackling future obstacles
- Not afraid to challenge her own perceptions of herself and the world around her
- Always finds new ways to enjoy life
- Doesn't wait for the perfect opportunity to come along but rolls up her sleeves and makes the most out of opportunities that come her way
- Embraces her power to change and experience new things at any age

TAKE ON THE DARE

Take a few minutes right now and get started on your Dream Self List. But more important, dare yourself to find ways to make these qualities part of your daily life and your daily actions.

_____

_____

_____

_____

_____

_____

Let Your Inner Daring Female Shine Through

D F A Daring Female may not like everything about herself, but she won't ever be caught trying to be like someone else. Enjoy yourself and all of the unique qualities that make you *you*. Don't rob the people around you of the chance to know what you're really like. Madonna said it right (and I know you won't dare to disagree with a Daring Female like her): Express yourself! Have strong opinions, express them often, and live a colorful and exciting life. Here are a few ideas for how to go about getting in touch with your innermost Daring Female and bringing her out for the world to see.

Dare to Love Your Quirks and Imperfections

Your thorns are the best parts of you.

—MARIANNE MOORE, AMERICAN POET

I couldn't think of a more daring way to start this chapter than by sharing a few of my own quirks and imperfections. To say that this list is incomplete is an understatement that would make anyone who knows me burst into laughter. Here goes:

- When I want something badly enough, I drive myself and everyone around me absolutely nuts trying to make it happen.

- My bottom and top teeth don't line up despite, or perhaps because of, various versions of funky-looking braces I wore as a teenager.
- I'm a neat freak and can't go to sleep if there are newspapers piled on the coffee table or there is a mess in my closet.
- I like cheesy eighties movies and occasionally listen to really bad pop music.

At various points in my life I've gone to great lengths to cover up these qualities and habits, often with great success. In many photographs I display a carefully constructed smile that just happens to conceal most of my bottom teeth. And while I was in high school, before my friends came over I'd make my room look messy by throwing around papers and clothes because that's what I thought was the cool thing to do. These are just a few examples of my ridiculous efforts to become more like the people around me and more like an image I'd built for myself. But really, who cares if my bottom teeth don't line up with my top teeth? Absolutely no one, and especially not the many people who never noticed this slight dental imperfection until I pointed it out to them. And I bet my friends wouldn't have thought less of me if they knew the true extent of my obsession with organization and neatness (and I'm sure that as much as I tried to be cool by being messy, I didn't create enough of a mess to fool too many of them). I don't think I ever had a eureka moment when I realized that the many quirks and imperfections I was trying to conceal made me memorable. Over time I began to embrace these quirks rather than hide them, and the sense of freedom this gave me to just live my life and not worry about sticking to a certain image was incredibly addictive.

Dare to love your quirks and imperfections! Whether it's a funny curve to your nose, your obsession with wearing stripes, or your inability to order in a restaurant in fewer than twenty minutes, these qualities are part of what makes you the awesome one-in-a-million Daring Female that you are. Embrace with all your might the distinctive things about you and leave your unmistakably special mark on the world. Trust me, you'll be doing more than just yourself a favor. Imagine a world in which all people have the same nose, wear pastels without patterns, and spend precisely two and a half minutes ordering at a restaurant—definitely an unbearably boring place I doubt you'd ever want to set your foot in.

And yet, as wonderful as it is to be ourselves, many of us go to great lengths to get rid of or hide our funky little quirks and imperfections. Maybe it's because we genuinely hate some of them, feel more comfortable not sharing our idiosyncrasies with the world, or are sure that people will think more of us if they don't know certain aspects of our personalities. While all of these might be perfectly legitimate reasons, they pale in comparison to the most important reason you should let go of your preconceptions: It's a lot more fun that way! Embracing your quirks, imperfections, and idiosyncrasies, instead of fighting or concealing them, frees up a huge amount of energy, allowing you to enjoy your life and do whatever you want with it.

When you're up-front about who you are, your chances of meeting people with whom you can form honest relationships get astronomically higher. This really hit home for me while I was talking to my friend about her on-again, off-again relationship with a great guy she really likes. I've always thought that he was right for her and could never understand why things weren't working out between them. He seemed to be in love with her and was an all-around wonderful guy. But every time they'd get romantically involved, my friend would eventually back off. When I recently suggested for the tenth time (as only an annoying friend can) that he might be the guy for her, she finally gave me an answer that made sense: He wasn't the right guy because he didn't really care about all her little quirks and idiosyncrasies. My friend is the least organized person I know; she has a set routine of running around her room looking for things at the last minute, as she tries to make it on time to a meeting or appointment (almost never happens). She is an endearing klutz who drops things, including food, on her clothes, making it pretty easy to tell what she had for lunch every day. She has an infectious laugh and a quirky sense of humor. And it was these and other seemingly insignificant qualities, *her* qualities, that this great guy didn't seem to value. They didn't bother him, she said, but they weren't part of what attracted him to her and she couldn't have a relationship with someone who didn't love her for who she was, including her klutziness and quirky sense of humor. She was so right I couldn't believe I hadn't realized it before.

So dare to be you, all of your wonderful and funky quirks intact. There's no better way to live a free life and have a ton of fun along the way!

A FEW DARING FEMALE QUIRKS AND IMPERFECTIONS

- Speaks and walks a hundred miles an hour
- Likes to do everything herself
- Can't sit in one place for long periods of time
- Tries to put a spin on even the most mundane daily activities
- Needs to maximize every moment and experience
- Has a loud, often raucous laugh
- Is stubborn and annoyingly tenacious
- Prefers to take a longer way to get somewhere as long as it's new and unexplored
- Is unpredictable
- Always has to express her opinion

TAKE ON THE DARE

Jot down three of your most wonderful quirks and imperfections. Dare to love them, not hide them, and enjoy yourself and your life!

_____

_____

_____

_____

_____

_____

Dare to Learn How to Do Something Amazingly Well and Show It Off

DARE-METER

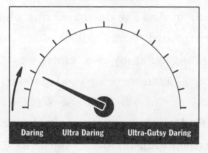

Daring   Ultra Daring   Ultra-Gutsy Daring

We only do well the things we like doing.

—COLETTE, FRENCH NOVELIST

Somewhere in your attic is a box filled with trophies, diplomas, ribbons, and other reminders of your accomplishments from when you were younger. I bet every time you open this box, your mouth stretches into the widest smile as you remember how terrific it felt to win your local equestrian competition or to have your secret-recipe gooseberry muffins place second in the town's muffin competition or to be the goalie of the high school soccer team that went to the state finals. Being great at something and being recognized for it feels incredibly empowering—it's like a super-strong triple shot of confidence in your morning coffee.

I don't know about you, but for me the feeling is addictive. I love it so much that every achievement does only one thing: It inspires and pushes me to do more, to aim higher and try harder, to learn how to do something well and feel amazing doing it. And I've discovered that while it's really nice to be recognized for my skills and accomplishments, nothing feels as good as my own respect for what I do and the confidence I gain from being good at something.

Okay, so I'm lying a little. To be completely honest, it feels really good when other people value and recognize my skills and accomplishments. When the books that my husband and I published through our little publishing company got a few positive reviews from publications that don't often review books from small presses, we were elated. *We* knew that the books were good, and often we'd go to Barnes & Noble, look at them on the shelf, and glow with pride about what we'd helped to create. But we glowed even more once a few authorities in the publishing world recognized what we'd done. As soon as we got the reviews we hit the phones and our e-mail to let parents, friends, and anyone we could contact know about our accomplishment; getting their congratulations made us feel even more confident that we could keep our company going.

We all have egos, and part of the euphoria associated

with achievement has to do with other people recognizing us for it. It's a natural human desire, and there's nothing wrong with it except for one thing—if you try to achieve or succeed at something solely to gain the admiration of other people. The only person you should be aiming to impress with your accomplishments is yourself; everything else is gravy. Most of us are our own toughest critics and judges, so if you don't value what you're trying to do, it won't matter much if others do.

Dare to learn to do something amazingly well and show it off! Think about what skills you'd like to gain, what you'd like to accomplish, and lay out a plan to go for it. It could be something to do with your job—say, learning how to create kick-ass presentations or mastering new technology. Look for your niche, that set of skills you want to learn in your job, and get really, really good at it. Besides the fact that these skills will help you succeed in your career (I'm going to stay away from giving career advice in this book, but numerous experts will tell you that having a specialty will help you stand out and progress in any organization), they will make you feel confident and bring that glow to your face when others recognize them.

Getting really good at something might lead you in a new life or career direction entirely. When talking to different women about this book I was introduced to Susie Galvez. She has always been interested in makeup. When she was just eight years old she mastered the skill of applying makeup by helping her mother, who couldn't see well.

Susie enjoyed seeing her mom smile because her mom liked how she looked. This feeling stayed with Susie as she grew up and got on with her life. While she pursued a career in sales, Susie kept thinking about how great she felt when she used makeup to make her mom and the other women in her family feel better about themselves. So when the company where she worked was sold, Susie decided that it was now or never for her to pursue her real interest. She went to school to become a licensed esthetician and bought a struggling spa. Susie used her passion and talent to turn the spa into a successful business, and now she gets to spend her days doing what she loves by helping people look their best. Susie told me that she thinks she gets a bigger charge than her clients do when they glow with confidence at how great they look. (You can learn more about Susie and her spa at www.faceworksdayspa.com.)

Learning how to do something well and showing it off doesn't necessarily have to do with embarking on a new career path. It's as exhilarating and fulfilling, if not more, to do this in other areas of your life. Do you like to paint? Take a class, work hard, paint like a madwoman, and raise your painting skills to a new level. Then fill your apartment (or house, if you're lucky enough to have one) with your art for your family, friends, and guests to marvel at. Or maybe you've always wanted to learn how to cook up a mean lamb stew? Hole up in your kitchen for a few days, armed with the best recipe books and ingredients. Try the recipes ten times, and once you've mastered your creations, invite as many people over for a feast as your dining room can handle.

Being awesome at something feels great and empowering, whether it's whipping up the most incredible passion fruit mousse or creating funky furniture designs. Choose an interest or skill you already have, take it to a whole new level, and don't be shy about sharing it with the world. Not only will you feel the amazing glow of being recognized for your achievement, but you'll be able to share it with other people. Could you ask for a more ideal combination?

DARING FEMALE IDEAS FOR SHOWING OFF

* Send your handmade cards to all of your family and friends for the holidays.
* Play the tape of your piano performance at your next get-together, and when someone asks who the great performer is, let them in on your secret and enjoy the moment.
* Show off your newly gained skills by ordering in French at a French restaurant.
* Copy your boss on an e-mail to a colleague that contains your latest and greatest presentation to the client.
* Trust your skill at scoping out a problem and coming up with a plan to solve it by volunteering to take the first crack at a tough assignment at work.
* Wear a daring outfit that shows off your newly buff body at your friend's party and don't say anything but "thank you!" when the compliments start pouring in.

TAKE ON THE DARE

Write down a few things you want to learn really well or skills you want to gain or improve, and dare to go for them. Make them part of your life and show them off to the world!

_____

_____

_____

_____

_____

_____

Dare to Be More Creative

DARE-METER

When I can no longer create anything I'll be done for.
—COCO CHANEL, FRENCH FASHION DESIGNER

One day while Lisa, my dental hygienist, was getting my teeth in order, I noticed some paintings on the wall that I hadn't seen before. I'd been coming to Lisa for many years and knew that she was a fan of art and even represented several local artists. So once my teeth were sparkling clean, I asked her which of the artists had painted the works. To my surprise, it turned out that it wasn't one of her artists, but Lisa herself. After being around art and artists for a while she got the urge to paint and started creating some wonderful abstract paintings.

I felt a connection with Lisa that day that I never thought I'd have with someone who hurts my teeth twice a year. Not because I too paint from time to time, but because I know that I couldn't get through my days and weeks of work and routine and errands without the escape of my creative pursuits. When Lisa talked about art, her face lit up, and I realized that I felt exactly the same way whenever I was immersed in one of my creative projects.

Dare to be more creative! You don't have to be a writer to write or an artist to paint, and writing and painting are only two ways to express yourself creatively. Here are some suggestions to get your creative juices going:

- **Start small**. Try to do something creative once a week or once a month. Cook dinner with exotic ingredients you've never used. If your family makes funny faces when you serve the meal, tell them that you're just expanding their eating horizons. They'll come to appreciate it even if they don't like it at first. Or make a small creative gift for someone. If it's Valentine's Day, how about buying some nice paper and creating your own set of Love Coupons? Go wild! You'll soon discover that your creative gifts are remembered and appreciated more than any other fancy-shmancy gifts you could find in a store.

- **Don't wait for a lightbulb to go off**. Creative ideas are more like treasures at the bottom of the ocean than like lightbulbs:

You have to swim around for a while, explore all around you, and go in many different directions before you spot the right idea. Give yourself the time and freedom to explore your ideas and don't get frustrated if you can't come up with something right away. For example, if you've decided to make your own creative holiday cards for your family and friends, take a trip to your local craft store and browse around for interesting materials you could use to make your cards truly distinctive. Try a few different combinations and don't worry if you can't find one that you love right away. Also, make sure to check out the holiday cards that the store carries; they can give you some new ideas to try out on your own.

· **Have a Creative Ideas Journal**. Write down any and all inspirations that you get. Don't discount any just because they seem improbable or silly. They aren't, and many might be detours on the way to your next grand idea.

· **Go to places that inspire you**. I read an article once in which the author Lisa Dierbeck talked about going to the library to find inspiration for her own work as a writer. At the library she finds herself surrounded by silence and thousands of books; her imagination is free to explore new ideas and directions she might not otherwise have considered. Sitting in your office or your house and staring at the wall isn't going to help, so get out there and let the world around you inspire your creativity.

· **Try**. Try to do new things, make new things, think about new things, expose yourself to new things. Sticking to what you know is safe and feels comfortable, but it's not the best way to come up with ideas and spice up your creative life. If you've never painted but always wanted to try, give it a shot! Set aside time one night each week to paint and don't treat it as something you can put off. If you usually hang out with the same set of friends, make some new friends who are quite different from you. You might experience a whole new side of life and yourself. You can meet new people by taking a class, going to bookstore readings, or joining one of the many groups on www.Meetup.com (groups for everyone from film lovers to jewelry makers).

It doesn't matter how you're creative, as long as you do something that helps you express yourself in a more personal, distinctive, and interesting way. Some of us are more creative than others, but we all have ideas, inspirations, and individual styles. Dare yourself to let that inner creative being shine through more often and you'll find that life gets more colorful, fun, and fulfilling.

Too many of our day-to-day activities involve stuff that doesn't call for creativity (unless you're one of the lucky few who has a creative job that pays the bills). You have to find the energy and the time to express your creativity, daring yourself not to fear failure. Who cares if your cherry and mozzarella pie recipe turns out tasting like . . . well, cherry and mozzarella pie? You created something all your own, and that makes life so much more fun.

Banish forever the following words from your vocabulary: "I am just not creative." The other day I was telling a friend of mine about a gift I'd made for my husband. "Wow," she said, "I could never do something like that. I'm just not the creative type." Ugh! It's just not true— everyone can be creative in some way! You can try new things, express yourself in new ways, and not care about what anyone else thinks about your creative pursuits. Start small and keep going; being creative can get addictive!

Have fun, go wild, and leave your own wonderfully creative mark on this world.

DARING FEMALE IDEAS FOR EXPLORING YOUR CREATIVITY

Sometimes we all need a little push, so here are a few ideas for creative projects that you can do when the urge strikes to do something a bit less ordinary. And if it doesn't strike soon, dare yourself to find it.

* Buy blank cards and write your own greetings—or make your own cards!
* Come up with fun date ideas that don't involve eating or seeing a movie.
* Write a poem by writing one line per day for one week.
* Make your own jewelry.
* Make up a holiday and celebrate it with your friends.
* Buy a few coloring books and be a kid again.
* Substitute a few unexpected ingredients for the tried and true ones in your favorite recipe.
* Make a collage out of unexpected objects like matchboxes, bottle caps, movie tickets, or old grocery lists.

TAKE ON THE DARE

Write down five ways in which you'd like to explore your creativity and dare to explore one this week. No matter how great or small, every creative effort is a breath of life and an amazing energy booster.

_____

_____

_____

_____

_____

Dare to *Not* Label Yourself

DARE-METER

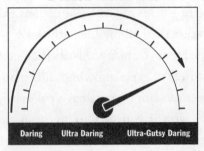

Daring   Ultra Daring   Ultra-Gutsy Daring

*It's a sad day when you find out that it's not accident or
time or fortune but yourself that kept things from you.*
—LILLIAN HELLMAN, AMERICAN DRAMATIST

I bet that even if you're an all-around free spirit you have
a few self-labels that guide how you live your life and
what you do with it. How about: "I'm a free spirit and
can't ever get organized." Or "I'm a free spirit, so I can't
commit to anything for a long time." Think about how you
perceive yourself and you'll find a few hidden—or not so
hidden—self-labels. If you're curious, here are a few that
I've applied to myself at different times in my life:

"I'm not a risk taker."

"I'm not adventurous."

"I'm super-organized and can't handle any chaos in my life."

Not all self-labels are bad. Some are genuine expressions of our personalities, and the more we understand ourselves, the better our chances for living lives that make us feel fulfilled and ecstatic. I'm definitely ultra-organized, and knowing this helps me create situations that allow me to succeed, rather than fill my life with chaos, which would drive me nuts. However, many self-labels do nothing except restrict the variety of experiences and directions we pursue. Because I never thought of myself as a risk taker, it took me longer than I wish it had to start my own company. I'm lucky to have had the guts to peel off that label, but I cringe thinking that I might have missed out on one of the most fulfilling, turbulent, and fascinating experiences in my life. When I think about what ultimately helped me redefine myself, I realize it was something very simple: I was so excited and passionate about starting our little publishing company that I never bothered to consider how it would fit with my idea of myself as someone who does not like risk.

Dare to *not* label yourself! Challenge your established ideas about the type of person you are and the life you're leading, and make sure you're living the way you want to. Self-labels don't just appear one day: We acquire them over time and are undoubtedly influenced by people around us. If your parents and teachers have always told you that you're not great at art/music/science/relationships/whatever, you'd have to be a pretty tough and independent soul (an ultra-Daring Female, that is!) to reject their judgments and not take them on as your own self-labels. Self-labels can be extremely sticky, so you'll need to summon all of your Daring Female power in order to remove them, to live a life in which you're free to choose what you do and how you do it.

While I was doing research for this book I got an e-mail from Diane, a woman whose story I thought was a great example of how sticky self-labels can be and how hard you have to work to detach them. While she was in high school, Diane wanted to become a journalist. Her family, on the other hand, thought that her mission in life was to find a well-to-do husband and become a stay-at-home mom. Diane listened to her family and went to school for secretarial studies, got married, and had two children. She enjoyed a lot about her life, but a few years later she realized that her notion of herself as someone who was always going to be a stay-at-home mom was limiting and was preventing her from getting as much out of her life as she wanted.

So Diane went back to school at the age of thirty and got a B.A. in media and communications. Several years later she went to work at Columbia University's Teachers College, where she earned a master's degree in international education development, and where she is now working on her Ph.D. Moving from being a full-time caretaker for her kids to pursuing other goals was an enormous challenge for Diane. At first, she felt guilty for not being able to spend as much time with her kids. Her family wasn't particularly supportive of the new priorities in her life, but she had to believe in herself and her desire to have a multifaceted life as an educated, working mother. The effort was worth it: Diane has experienced and learned things she never would have otherwise. She has gotten an amazing education, has found a fulfilling job that pays her to do things she loves, has traveled all over the world (learning many different languages along the way), and has remained a mother and a supportive friend to her growing kids the whole time.

Self-labels are different from simple likes or dislikes. For example, you might not enjoy big loud parties, but that doesn't make you antisocial. Self-labels are more all-encompassing: When you label yourself you define yourself as a certain kind of person. These definitions may limit the choices you make in your life and the diversity of experiences you seek out. The tricky thing about self-labels is that they can make life seem quite comfortable. If you've labeled yourself as someone who doesn't ever take the lead, then you probably rarely seize the initiative and save yourself the stress that often comes with being in charge of something. But you're missing out on the great excitement, satisfaction, and learning that taking a lead can bring and that's a shame. Have some guts to leave the comfort zone of your self-labels once in a while and you may find that you never want them back.

One of my friends was recently telling me about a guy she met online; they've really hit it off and have been dating for a few months. I didn't bring it up, but just last year, when I suggested that she try one of those online dating sites, she told me that she would never even consider it. She'd been complaining about not being able to meet enough new people, but said that she was a believer in fate. She was not someone who initiated conversations with strangers, especially strangers she met online. I don't know what will happen with her and this particular guy, but peeling off her self-label as someone who believes only in fate has already freed her up to meet people in many different ways and feel more in control of her life.

The less you limit yourself, the more widely you'll explore and the more chances you'll have to find things and meet people you really enjoy. Life is full of amazing experiences, opportunities, and wild turns, and every day is your chance to use your Daring Female freedom and gutsy power to explore as many of them as you can.

NON-DARING SELF-LABELS TO AVOID

- I'm not an art person.
- I'm not into dancing.
- I only like food that I can pronounce.
- I don't do all that new age stuff.
- I'm not into any traditional sports.
- I'm not someone who takes the lead.
- I'm not an outdoors person.
- I'm not the adventurous type.
- I don't travel to countries where English isn't spoken.
- I'm not a fun person.
- I'm not creative.
- I'm too old for this.
- I'm too young for this.
- I'm not a social person.
- I don't do anything unless I'm incredibly good at it.

TAKE ON THE DARE

Jot down a few of your self-labels and dare to be brutally honest and question how accurate they are. Don't be afraid to peel off more than a few and let yourself be free to experience as many parts of this ecstatic life as humanly possible.

_____

_____

_____

_____

_____

_____

Dare to Take Sides, but Be Ready to Switch

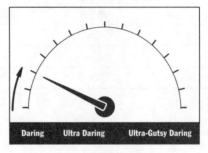

Better a false belief than no belief at all.
—GEORGE ELIOT, ENGLISH NOVELIST

Think of some of the most interesting and engaging people you know and I bet you'll find that they all share one characteristic: They have strong opinions and aren't afraid to share them. Sure, they might drive you crazy with beliefs that are diametrically opposed to yours, but you can't call them boring or dull. And I'll take interesting over dull any day. Wouldn't you?

In the interest of full disclosure, I should tell you that I have a personal bias toward people with strong opinions—I happen to be one of them. I have strong opinions about nearly everything I encounter in life, from politics to movies to food to people to shoelaces, and everything in between. You'd be hard-pressed to catch me saying that something is just okay: I either absolutely positively love it or I can't stand it with every fiber in my body. I have almost no ability to keep my mouth shut when during a conversation an issue comes up that I care about, regardless of whether I think others would agree or vehemently disagree with me (and I can tell you that this drives more than a few of my friends nuts). Why do I do this? Well, for one, I think it's my nature, and according to my parents I've been this way since I was born. I also think that having and expressing strong opinions makes me more interesting and fun to be around.

One of my good friends is a dynamite woman with whom I disagree on hundreds of things, from good TV shows (her favorite is one I refuse to watch) to food (I am a meat lover and she's an animal lover and a vegetarian) to germs (I wash my hands before I eat lunch, while she disinfects hers with an ultra-powerful special potion that comes in a bottle). She is strong, dynamic, and fun to be around— not the least because she's opinionated and fearless about letting the world know what she thinks. She lights up the room, and you just get this desire to talk to her and keep talking to her, whether you agree with what she's saying or want to rip your hair out because of it. I'm never bored around her and she brightens up even the grayest of days.

But while it's truly a Daring Female quality to have

strong opinions and not be timid about sharing them, I think it's even more daring to be willing to change your mind. Sometimes we hang on to the ideas and beliefs we've held for a long time as if they were our favorite security blanket; they make us feel safe and comfortable, so we bring them everywhere we go. Well, I suggest that you make it a habit to take some time and figure out if you genuinely care and believe in something or if you're hanging on to your opinions just because they've been with you for a while. Be open to hearing new ideas and changing your mind. Take as much as possible from your life experiences and the people you meet. If what you learn makes you change your mind about something you had believed in, even if it's something you've always held as an absolute, then let yourself change. Changing your mind doesn't make you fickle—it makes you genuine and alive.

Dare to take sides, but be ready to switch! Dare to care about issues and causes and to speak out about things that matter to you. Challenge yourself to get out of the neutral zone; instead, learn enough to form a strong opinion one way or another. Make yourself and your life more interesting and exciting by saying what's on your mind, even to people who might disagree with you. Just don't forget to remain open to learning new ideas and changing your ways. I read an article once that talked about the fact that the older we get, the more established we become in our tastes. Apparently, after forty, we aren't likely to fall in love with a new kind of music or a new toothpaste. Well, I'm not forty yet, but boy, do I hope to prove them wrong! Live, absorb, experience, have definite opinions and views, and challenge yourself to be receptive to changing them, regardless of how set in your ways you may be. Have some fun with life!

Learning about different issues might lead you to realize that there are a few about which you care a lot. Being passionate about a certain cause feels really great and I think that it's absolutely necessary to living a meaningful and rich life. It's easy to get caught up in routines but remember that life is bigger than that. Take your passion and use it to spur you into taking an active role in your favorite cause. You can join an organization that supports your cause and invigorate it with your refreshing energy and commitment. Or if you can't find such an organization, start your own. This sounds daunting, but hey, you wouldn't be a gutsy Daring Female if you didn't take on such challenges. Think about the impact you can have, hold on to your passion for the cause, and give it all you've got. If you truly care about something, you will figure out how to organize people around it and promote your cause.

Here's a story to inspire you:

From the age of ten, Emily Spivack witnessed her mother's battle with recurring breast cancer. She initially tried to help out by taking care of her younger sister, doing chores, and staying out of trouble, but when the cancer returned, Emily decided she wanted to be more involved in her mom's recovery. She saw that her mom always felt better when she looked good and could wear fashionable, comfortable clothing. So Emily took it upon herself to help her mom find outfits that made her feel great and were comfortable to wear after her mastectomy and during chemotherapy. Being able to help her mom inspired Emily to start a nonprofit organization called Shop Well with You. Its mission is to help cancer survivors improve their body image and feel positive about their recovery. Emily received the funds to start her organization after winning the Business Plan Competition at Brown University, from which she graduated. She moved to New York City, and after months of tremendous effort and late nights, Shop Well with You was born. Emily's organization has allowed her passion for a cause to benefit thousands of women. As Shop Well with You grows, its mission and benefits will reach more and more cancer survivors and help them lead better lives. What an amazingly rewarding way for Emily to exercise her Daring Female power! (To learn more about Shop Well with You, check out the organization's Web site, www.shopwell withyou.org.)

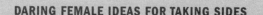

DARING FEMALE IDEAS FOR TAKING SIDES

Give your brain cells a workout and take some sides: Check out the issues below and think about where you stand on each. Some might intrigue you, some might bore you to tears, but all should be like a springboard that gets you thinking about ideas and issues you care about.

* **Politics** Do you consider yourself a liberal, a moderate, or a conservative? Why?
* **Environment** Would you stop going to your favorite restaurant if you discovered that it didn't recycle?
* **Family/Work** Would you sacrifice time with your family to pursue a job or an opportunity appealing to you?
* **Religion** Do you believe in God?
* **People** Do you think people are inherently good or bad?
* **Freedom** Are you willing to sacrifice some civil liberties for increased security?
* **Patriotism** Would you pay more for a product made in America or buy a cheaper product made abroad?
* **Homosexuality** How do you feel about gay/lesbian marriage?
* **Death penalty** Are you for or against it? Why?
* (Fill in the blank) is a cause you passionately care about.

TAKE ON THE DARE

Create a list of ideas or issues about which you have strong feelings and dare to express your thoughts loud and clear the next time a relevant conversation comes up. Better yet, put your effort where your mouth is: Find a local organization devoted to promoting this cause and join, adding your own vigor and energy.

_____

_____

_____

_____

_____

_____

Have
No
Fear

D**F** You might get lucky and stumble into exciting experiences and too-good-to-be-true opportunities just by chance. But most of the time, it takes guts—and a real leap of faith—to live an exciting and invigorating life. A Daring Female isn't superhuman; she feels nervous and scared and anxious about making big changes or pursuing things that are completely new. But she trusts her gut and believes in her ability to take away something from every situation (even if it's just the knowledge that she never wants to be in that situation again). She welcomes adventure and seeks out ways to re-create her life when she's stuck in a rut. And if you need some inspiration to do more of that yourself—quick, turn the page and read on!

Dare to Ignore the Naysayers

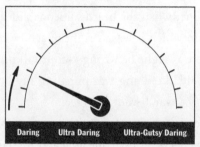

*If Rosa Parks had taken a poll before she sat down in the
bus in Montgomery, she'd still be standing.*

—MARY FRANCES BERRY,

AMERICAN ACTIVIST AND EDUCATOR

A couple of years ago I worked with a colleague who was
super-smart. Whenever I'd talk to her about a project
that had stumped me, she'd usually come up with
some approaches that I hadn't considered. I appreciated her
input when we talked about work, but I'd always leave our
conversations feeling strangely deflated. I couldn't figure
out why until one day I came to her with an idea for a busi-

ness I thought would be fun to start. I was really excited about it, but she came up with dozens of reasons as to why it would never work. I'm sure many of them were right on and her arguments were, as usual, very intelligent. It was her tone that made her message sound like a recording: "There's no way this silly idea is ever going to work!" It was as if she had dismissed my idea as soon as she heard it.

And suddenly it hit me: I was dealing with a naysayer. Her first instinct when she heard someone's idea or plan was to find ways in which it wasn't right or achievable. It didn't matter if she was right or wrong—after talking to her, the last thing I felt like doing was pursuing my business idea. This was *not* the way I wanted to feel.

After that incident I decided I'd be better off putting some distance between my colleague and myself. I'm all for hearing opposing opinions and think that there's a lot of value in getting a range of views on the same issue or idea. However, when someone makes you feel discouraged or deflated with his or her naysayer attitude, then it's time to run, not walk, away from that person. People give advice and share their thoughts in various ways. You can definitely find people who do this in a positive, constructive, and encouraging fashion that inspires you to go after what you want, instead of deflating your excitement and discouraging you from the start.

Dare to ignore the naysayers in your life! You know who they are—we all have some friends, acquaintances, or coworkers who find a way to put down an idea or poke holes in a plan or a dream. Some of them do this because they let their own insecurities take over; people who have confidence in themselves and in what they are doing rarely discourage others from pursuing something they care about. It's sad to think that someone might want to sabotage your success, but it happens. Some naysayers are genuinely trying to be helpful, without realizing that their naysayer attitude is anything but. It doesn't matter: If after talking to someone you feel discouraged instead of feeling energized, stay away or ignore the negativity of that person's message. Why? Because:

- Life is too short to hang around people who discourage you.
- There's a good possibility that the naysayers are completely wrong.
- If you want something badly enough you'll find a way to make it happen, even if you have to try a hundred times.
- People's motivations for telling you that your idea or plan won't work aren't always noble; many are influenced by envy or greed.
- Your chances of reaching your goals and fulfilling your dreams are much greater if you surround yourself with those who want you to succeed and help you with their positive energy and helpful ideas.

When Mary Spio decided to give up her successful career as a deep space scientist to launch a national magazine for singles, everyone thought she was nuts. Her family members, friends, and colleagues told her she was throwing away a good thing and they were disappointed by her choice. Many thought she'd completely lost it and turned into an actual mad scientist. But Mary was set on her course and determined to pursue it. After she worked on a NASA project that sent probes into space to find intelligent life, Mary realized she wanted to create something that would help people connect and communicate right here on Earth. When the naysayers spoke out, Mary was not discouraged: She'd had to battle naysayers before when no one believed that she could become a space scientist. She had ignored the naysayers, graduating first in her male-dominated class, where, incidentally, she used the same lab station as Eileen Collins, the first female space shuttle commander. And she successfully ignored the naysayers this time around as well. What Mary believes helped her make a dramatic career change, pursue her interest, and launch what has since become a popular magazine, called *One 2 One Living*, was the conviction that the only person she could really trust in determining when she would succeed or fail was herself. She didn't ignore all the advice and input she received. But she trusted herself and her gut above all else: She wanted to make her vision come to life and was willing to work as hard as she needed to do it. (You can check out the fruits of Mary's labor on the magazine's Web site, www.one2onemag.com.)

Sometimes you might lose your confidence and determination if the people you trust tell you you won't succeed. You've got to listen to your gut instinct and use your Daring Female power to separate the constructive and helpful criticism from naysayer discouragement. If you feel good about something and get excited at the thought of doing it, that's your gut talking, so listen up! You decide whether you can make something happen in your life. Sure, your efforts might not pay off immediately (or even for a long time), but you'll find a way if you want it badly enough. Tell the naysayers to step aside and seek out people who can give you the advice and support to help you reach your goals.

DARING FEMALE PROS AT IGNORING NAYSAYERS

- **Marilyn Monroe** was dropped from her contract by 20th Century Fox in 1947, because the head of production thought she was unattractive.
- **Lucille Ball** was told that she had no acting talent and was too quiet and shy to become an actress.
- **Katie Couric** was informed by the president of CNN that her voice was too irritating and high-pitched to read headline news reports.
- **Allison Janney** was told that because of her height (she is six feet tall) she would not make it in TV or film.
- **Ayn Rand** was told in 1943 that there was no audience for *The Fountainhead* and it would not sell.
- **Margaret Mitchell's** *Gone with the Wind* was rejected by publishers thirty-eight times.

TAKE ON THE DARE

List a few naysayers in your life and dare to be strong enough to ignore their negative attitude or spend less time with them altogether.

_____

_____

_____

_____

_____

_____

Dare to Take Life Detours

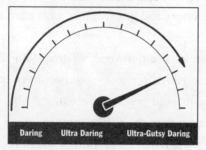

DARE-METER

Daring   Ultra Daring   Ultra-Gutsy Daring

*Adventure can be an end in itself. Self-discovery is the
secret ingredient that fuels daring.*
—GRACE LICHTENSTEIN, AMERICAN WRITER

*S*et goals. Know where you're going in life. Have a direction.
This advice is constantly drilled into us by our parents, teachers, counselors, and countless self-help books
and magazine articles. In principle, I have absolutely nothing against it. I'm a goal-oriented person who has taken
advice like this to heart from as early an age as I can
remember. My goals and direction in life have changed
more than a few times, but I'm rarely caught without them.

But I would be in trouble if along the way I hadn't dared myself to take a few detours from my grand life plan. I would never have discovered that writing, not pursing a career as a corporate lawyer, is what makes me ecstatic. I would never have felt the fear and excitement of quitting a well-paying and secure job to launch my very own company. I cringe thinking what my life would have been like if I'd stuck to my long-term plans and not allowed myself to follow my interests and gut feelings more than a few times in the past few years.

Dare to take life detours! Whether you have a grand plan for where you'd like to see yourself in twenty years or can hardly plan your week, give yourself the freedom to have experiences that you'd like but that don't necessarily fit neatly into the general direction of where you're headed. As you go through life, you are constantly learning and changing. You owe it to yourself to take a step off the path you're following to make sure that it's truly something that makes you happy. If, say, you want to go back to school or try out a new career path, take some time and figure out how you can do this without completely turning your life upside down. The beauty of a detour is that if you want, you can always go back to your original path in life. You can go back to school part-time or network and conduct informational interviews in another industry to get a taste of what working in that field is like. If you enjoy your detour, then you will have more confidence in changing your life and pursuing your new goal with full force—going back to school full-time or applying for jobs in a different industry.

A few years ago I was looking to hire a copy editor to help us out in our publishing business. One résumé I received looked particularly strong except for one thing: The woman applying for the job took six years to finish college. Her résumé was filled with impressive jobs and she appeared to be an ambitious person. When we spoke on the phone, I asked her to tell me about her college experience and why she took six years to graduate. It turned out that she took two years off to help her friend start a shoe company. She had never thought of taking time off from college, but her friend, who had already graduated, didn't want to wait. This young woman had so much fun learning how to build a business that when she graduated she decided to pursue a career working with small companies instead of going to graduate school. She was happy with her choice and thankful she had the guts to take a detour from her life plan and explore something new and unfamiliar. (We did hire her, by the way, and she did an awesome job.)

Not only does taking a detour make life more interesting and colorful, but it's also a great way to find out if what you're after is truly something that you want. We sometimes have to get away from what we're doing in order to be able to evaluate how we feel about it and whether we want to stick with it or make a change. For example, your highly structured work environment in a large company might be driving you crazy (along with your overbearing boss). So you take a life detour and become an independent consultant, thereby getting all the freedom you want and becoming your own boss. After a few years of working around the clock, doing everything from luring clients to changing printer cartridges, you decide that you'd actually prefer to be part of a company, where you can focus on doing your work and not worry about filing your taxes or getting the phones to work. If you hadn't taken a life detour, you might not have realized that while some parts of your corporate job frustrate you, the corporate world is actually the right place for you to be. In other words, taking a detour from your life can help you appreciate your life as it is. And that's a wonderful feeling!

Sometimes taking a detour from trying to reach your life goals can turn out to be just the way to reach them. Alexandra Allred has wanted to be a writer since she was a little girl. At one point she wrote a few movie scripts but couldn't get anywhere with them. So she put her desire to become a published writer on the back burner and got on with her life: college, marriage, a baby. One day she was watching a bobsledding competition on ESPN; she waited for the women's performances to follow the men's, and eventually realized that there were no female competitors. This made no sense to her, so she called up the Bobsled Federation and asked why women didn't compete. She was told that the sport was considered too dangerous for women. Appalled, Alexandra told them to put her name down as someone who wanted to try it. To her surprise, she got a call a month later asking for her athletic résumé. The only thing she could put on it was competitive martial arts, but she ended up being invited to the bobsledding camp at the Olympic Training Center. Without any experience, still nursing her baby, and not knowing what she was getting into, Alexandra went.

Talk about a huge life detour—never in her wildest dreams did Alexandra imagine that she'd be training to compete in bobsledding. She was never the best athlete, but she worked her butt off, impressed the coaches with her go-getter attitude, and was invited back to the camp several more times, each time returning in better shape than before. In 1998 Alexandra won the U.S. Nationals in bobsledding (women were finally allowed to compete) and was named Athlete of the Year by the U.S. Olympic Committee. And she was four and a half months pregnant when she won!

Her success in sports opened many doors for Alexandra, and she used this opportunity to pursue her enduring passion for writing. Her first book was published in 1996, many years and an unexpected detour after she put her desire to become a writer on hold. She now has more than twelve books in print, many of which are about sports. Recently she was asked by *Sports Illustrated* to try out for a women's football team and then write about it. Did she do it? Do you really have to ask? As a truly Daring Female, Alexandra has learned one amazing thing from her experiences: "Because I am willing to try new things, even things completely out of my scope of knowledge, I am living a dream!"

Taking detours from your life plan is definitely not for the faint of heart. You're exploring unfamiliar territory, your family and friends look at you funny or worry about you, and since you're not following a detailed plan the chances are high you may get lost. This is when you have to summon up your Daring Female power and go for it anyway. You never know where the detour might lead you. For example, you might research a spa business and find that this is truly something you'd like to seriously pursue or you might realize that going to a spa from time to time satisfies your curiosity just fine. But if you don't take a detour you'll never know, and not knowing what makes you thrilled to live your life every day is not an option for a Daring Female.

THE DARING FEMALE LIFE DETOURS COMPASS

Use this quick guide to figure out which life detours you dare to pursue and where you want to go once you do.

1. Write down three things you've always wanted to do in your life but that don't fit into your current life plan.
2. Rank each on a scale of 1 to 3 (1 = least, 3 = most) of how much you'd like to pursue it.
3. Now rank each on a scale of 1 to 3 (1 = most difficult, 3 = least difficult) of how difficult it will be for you to do it.
4. Choose a life detour that has the highest combined rating on your ultra non-complicated scale (for each, add the first rank to the second). This way you're balancing your desire to take a certain detour with the challenge of taking it at this very moment in your life.
5. Write down three specific steps you would need to take to embark on your detour.
6. Dare to pursue your life detour, and as you do, check your detour compass from time to time and write down what you like and don't like about your new experience.
7. Spend some time thinking about whether you'd like to make this detour part of your life or if you're satisfied with embarking on it from time to time.
8. If you decide that you want to turn this detour into the main path of your life, dare to create a plan for how to do it, and use all of your Daring Female guts and power to make it happen.

TAKE ON THE DARE

Take some time and think about where you're headed in your life and what detours you'd like to explore. Dare yourself to take at least one soon; you never know where it will lead you.

_____

_____

_____

_____

_____

_____

Dare to Take Risks If You Can Live with the Worst-Case Scenario

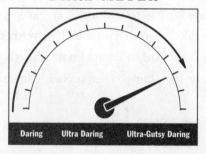

DARE-METER

| Daring | Ultra Daring | Ultra-Gutsy Daring |

If you risk nothing, you risk everything.

—GEENA DAVIS, ACTRESS

Several months after my husband and I decided to start a publishing company out of our one-bedroom apartment we got our first shot of reality: It was going to be a lot harder than we thought. Our sales numbers were lower than we expected, our expenses were much higher, and we had to decide whether to keep going or to cut our losses and quit. If we kept going, we'd risk losing all of our life savings, which we used to start the company. If we quit now, we'd protect some of our savings (the money that was still in the bank), but we'd feel like we were giving up on our dream of having our own company. However, even if we failed, we'd know that we had followed our passion, given it all we could, and learned some amazing things along the way. We thought about our worst-case scenario and knew that while it would be painful, we would manage to survive it. Realizing this made our choice of what to do clear, although anything but easy: We had to take a risk and keep going.

Dare to take risks if you can live with the worst-case scenario! It's hard to always know what the worst-case scenario will be like, but you can probably imagine it:

- You don't get that job.
- Your business fails.
- Five people show up to your new bakery.
- The critics pan your book.
- The guy you ask out says no.
- You can't stand the guy you asked out.

At first look, the worst-case scenario for each risk you're considering might seem awful, not something you think you can live with. But except for a few serious situations in life, most worst-case scenarios are unbearable for only a short while, after which you can find ways to make it through them and learn something in the process. Consider, for example, the worst-case scenarios from above and ways you might get through them with flying colors:

You don't get that job.	You still have your old job and can look for another one. After looking through the online listings you find an open position that you like even better.
Your business fails.	You've gained life experiences that you can use in your work for another company or to make your next venture successful.
Five people show up to your new bakery.	You invite all of your family and friends over for free dessert and brainstorm creative marketing ideas to get the word out about your amazing chocolate chip cookies.
The critics pan your book.	You realize that many successful authors have been panned by critics at one time or another and start working on your next book.
The guy you asked out says no.	You sulk for a while and then use the money you would've spent on a date to take your best friend for a girls' night out, which turns out to be outrageously fun.
You can't stand the guy you asked out.	You survive through the evening, rent your favorite movie on the way home, and get the bad-guy vibes out of your system with a tub of popcorn.

You *can* live through most worst-case scenarios. Be aware of them, but don't dwell on them. If there's something you really want, however challenging, improbable, or tough it might be, dare yourself to go for it. Go for that impossible-to-get job, write your version of the next great American novel, change the way you look, anything, as long as you want it badly enough. You only live once—if you don't do it now, then when?

Taking a risk is tough, scary, uncertain, and sometimes very lonely. It isn't always fun, it's never easy, and you should do it only if what you're after is something you really want. If it is, then you'll find the energy to push yourself and work toward your goal and find people who will support you.

If the thought of taking a risk is still too daunting, take some time to think about the consequences of not taking a risk. Will you look back and wish that you'd found enough guts to do it? Will you feel like you settled for something instead of going for what you really want? Will you drown in an ocean of "woulda/coulda/shoulda"? Think about it and you might realize that taking a risk and failing is more invigorating than playing it safe.

DARING FEMALE RISK TAKERS

- **Cameron Tuttle** quit her job, embarked on a 100,000-mile road trip, and used it as inspiration to write her bestseller, *The Bad Girl's Guide to the Open Road,* which gave birth to the flourishing Bad Girl brand.
- **Dineh Mohajer**, unhappy with the boring nail polish on store shelves, started mixing up her own funky polish in her kitchen, and soon was running her own successful cosmetics company, Hard Candy.
- **Ellen DeGeneres** came out as a lesbian on national TV, putting her reputation and future job offers at risk. Her humor still rocks and so does her amazingly popular talk show.
- **Meg Whitman** took the job as CEO of eBay, perhaps the most successful Internet company, at the seeming peak of its success. eBay has grown every year since she's taken over.
- **Oprah** decided to pursue her passion and become a news anchor when few black women or men were given the job. Her daytime show has been number one in rankings for endless years and she now runs a multi-mega-million-gazillion-dollar media empire, including one of the most successful magazines in the industry.

TAKE ON THE DARE

Choose a risk you're considering taking and write out some worst-case scenarios that might result if you do. For each worst-case scenario list a few things that will help you deal with it. After you're done, take a deep breath, trust your gut, and dare to take a risk!

_____

_____

_____

_____

_____

_____

Dare to Revel in the Awesome-Case Scenario

DARE-METER

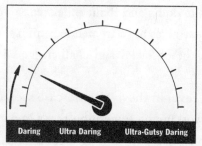

There are times when life surprises one, and anything can happen, even what one hoped for.

— ELLEN GLASGOW, AMERICAN NOVELIST

In college my best friend and I would often spend hours talking about all the things we were going to do in our lives. We'd get so excited about the future and had no doubt about being able to make it all happen. Perhaps we were naive and silly. But even then we knew how difficult and even improbable many of our plans were, yet we just didn't care: Spending time reveling in the awesome-case scenarios of our lives was a source of great energy, excitement, and optimism.

After we graduated, my friend and I ended up on opposite ends of the country and hardly get to see each other anymore. And maybe because of the distance, we've stopped having those talks about our grandiose future. I miss them and the pure excitement that came with them. These days I'm on my own when it comes to suspending reality for a bit and indulging in huge, incredible, and often unlikely dreams about the future. For me, getting excited about what I'm doing and about the potential for success is like a drug—it gives me a tremendous high that helps me get through the obstacles and challenges as I pursue my goals.

Dare to revel in the awesome-case scenario! Whenever you're working on something that's important to you or trying to realize one of your dreams or goals, stretch your imagination and think about the best possible scenario for how things can turn out. Don't worry about being realistic or grounded—many of us are too realistic and grounded, often forgetting to have wild dreams and believe that we can actually make them happen. If you're auditioning for a part, believe that you'll floor the director with your incredible performance. If you're entering a competition or a contest, envision yourself doing better than you ever have and winning the top prize. If your show is opening at a gallery, imagine that it will be a huge success, with the top critics fighting over who will interview you first. Whatever you do, don't sell yourself short—you need to aim for the sky in order to have a shot at reaching it. And if you can't imagine yourself realizing your dreams successfully, then who can?

Along the way to achieving your dreams and goals, there will be challenges and unpleasant surprises you could never have predicted at the beginning. You will get scared, feel overwhelmed, and have days when you doubt that you can ever succeed. If you're lucky, you'll have support and encouragement from your family and friends, but no encouragement can compare with your own belief in your ability to succeed. The buzz you get from thinking about the best possible outcome is the fuel you need to help you on the often difficult road toward your dreams.

If you're going to chase a dream, it should be because you're passionate about it and willing to work incredibly hard. Whatever obstacles you encounter along the way, make sure they are not the ones you yourself created by not believing in the best possible outcome. Before you can succeed, you need to imagine yourself succeeding and believe in that image.

You might wonder if you aren't setting yourself up for disappointment by indulging in thoughts of the most awesome-case scenario. What happens when you've worked as hard as you can and still find yourself far from the great outcome you'd envisioned? You'll probably feel disappointed, which is perfectly normal. And while disappointment is no fun, it's not nearly as bad as thinking you should've reached higher and dreamed bigger, or wondering what would have happened if you had.

No one can offer you the exact recipe that will guarantee you'll realize your dreams. Whatever ingredients you choose—hard work, persistence, patience—always mix in one part wild imagination and belief that the awesome-case scenario will happen. You owe it to yourself!

DARING FEMALE SUCCESS VOCABULARY

Here's your starter word kit to use when describing your goals and the dreams you one day hope to achieve. Don't dare chase your goals without it.

- Awesome
- Bigger than life
- Tremendous
- Astonishing
- Amazing
- Fabulous
- Extraordinary
- Incredible
- Grand
- Remarkable
- Breathtaking
- Fantastic
- Great
- Magnificent

TAKE ON THE DARE

Think of one of your life goals and dare to imagine the most incredible way in which you can possibly achieve it. Write it down and use it as your reminder to believe in your Daring Female ability to conquer all odds and succeed beyond your wildest dreams.

_____

_____

_____

_____

_____

_____

Dare to **Un**-intimidate Yourself

DARE-METER

Daring   Ultra Daring   Ultra-Gutsy Daring

Life shrinks or expands in proportion to one's courage.
—ANAÏS NIN, NOVELIST

When my agent called to say that a publisher in New York wanted to meet with me because they were interested in my book (yes, this very book you're reading), I jumped so high that I almost made a hole in the ceiling. But once I caught my breath and started to think about the actual meeting, I got nervous. The more I thought about it, the more reasons I came up with for why the publisher would not want to buy my book. After a few days I managed to intimidate myself into a state of complete nervousness.

I knew that I couldn't go into my meeting feeling this way—I had to go in with confidence, power, and a ton of oomph in my step. So I set out to un-intimidate myself. I like to analyze things to death, so I made up a list of all the reasons I thought the publisher wouldn't buy my book. Next to each I wrote a counterargument I could present if that reason came up in conversation. Here's a sample:

Intimidator	Un-Intimidator
I'm a first-time book author.	Although I've never written a book, I have tons of writing experience. I've written articles and columns and I've edited and rewritten all of the books published by our company.
I don't have a platform from which to promote my book.	Although I don't have an established platform, I understand the importance of promoting my book through every possible channel. I am a relentless worker with a passion for my book and I will commit to building a platform together with the publisher.

I can't tell you that after I'd made my list I didn't feel nervous—that would be a big lie! But once I had thought through the potential objections that the publisher might have and prepared great arguments to throw right back at them, I definitely felt more confident.

The meeting went really well. They brought up some of the issues I thought they would, but we also talked about many other things, such as who I thought would really like to read this book and what made me think of writing it. I realized that if I arrived at the meeting feeling intimidated and nervous, I would have risked not coming off as strong, charismatic, or confident. And that very lack of confidence, instead of all the other things I worried about, might have tanked the deal.

Dare to *un*-intimidate yourself! It's easy to become intimidated when you're faced with a tough situation, an important meeting, or a task that you've not tackled before. But we're stronger than our natural reactions and have tremendous power to un-intimidate ourselves. The first and probably most important step is believing that you will conquer your nerves. Once you do that, you're on a roll. I suggest that you make a list of all the reasons you feel intimidated and think about each one carefully: What arguments or points can you come up with to counter it? This might take some creativity, but hey, you're a Daring Female! After you come up with your un-intimidators, let them sink in for a while. They won't work unless you genuinely believe in them.

Remember that when you're given an opportunity—to interview for a top position, to present a new idea to a client, to perform in front of an audience—someone thinks that you can do it. The trick is convincing *yourself* that you can. If you can't get rid of your anxieties entirely, try visualizing them as being locked away in a remote, hard-to-reach part of your mind. If you can do that, you'll be letting your true self come through full force and with confidence; this kind of attitude is more powerful than anything else in helping you move mountains and rock the world.

I find that the more I want something, the more I become emotionally invested in it and the harder I have to fight my nerves when I try to achieve it. Expect to be intimidated and nervous, don't beat yourself up for these feelings, and use your Daring Female power to un-intimidate yourself. Never forget that your emotions are under your control.

If reasoning with yourself is not your style, I dare you to conquer your intimidations in a more radical, head-on way. Instead of analyzing each situation or action that intimidates you, muster up all your Daring Female guts and power and just jump into it. Acknowledge your intimidation and even fear, accept that that's how you feel, and do it anyway. Even more than that, deliberately seek out situations that would normally intimidate you. If, for example, you'd rather have a root canal than speak in front of a large group of people, volunteer to deliver the next presentation to your client at work. Yes, your knees will feel weak, your palms will sweat, your heart will want to jump out of your chest, and you'll probably curse yourself for deciding to do this at all. But I bet that the more you confront your intimidations head-on, the more confident you'll become. You'll begin to realize that you are stronger than your fears.

This is what happened to Patricia Baronowski when she decided to finally conquer her fear of heights. While she lived a daring life in every other aspect, Patricia always felt burdened by her fear. So one day she made up her mind to do something about it . . . by going skydiving. Talk about confronting your intimidations in a radical way! But Patricia felt that she had to do it: If she could skydive, then standing on top of a tall ladder was never going to be an issue. So she literally jumped into it and went for a tandem skydive. The result? Not only did she overcome her fear of heights, but she fell in love with the sport and became a licensed skydiver, with 258 jumps under her belt and counting. After this, she knew that she could conquer anything!

Life is too sweet to go through it being afraid of taking actions just because they make you nervous. Acknowledge your intimidations, confront them in the way that works best for you, and feel the awesome high of having overcome them.

DARING FEMALE FORBIDDEN INTIMIDATIONS

- I can't ever do this.
- If I try this and fail, I'll be even more intimidated the next time.
- What if the publisher/boss/investor/critic doesn't like my work?
- I am too afraid to do this now, so I'll have to do it later.
- I've never done anything like this before.
- My friends don't think that I can do this.
- I'm not smart/strong/experienced enough to succeed.

TAKE ON THE DARE

Jot down three actions or situations that intimidate the living daylights out of you and create a short plan for how you'll confront each and attempt to free your life from it.

_____

_____

_____

_____

_____

_____

It's Your
Daring
Life

D F A Daring Female knows that she has got to *LIVE* every day of her life and not spend it bogged down by routines, worries, or fear of stepping beyond her boundaries. Better yet, she knows that it's up to her to live her life in the most interesting, meaningful, and enjoyable way. It may mean taking chances, kicking annoying habits, forgetting how old she is or what she is good or bad at. Or it may mean something completely different. Read on for a few ideas about how to shake up your life to make sure that you're getting as much out of every day as you possibly can.

Dare to Do Something You Don't Think You're Good at Once in a While

DARE-METER

You must do the thing you think you cannot do.

—ELEANOR ROOSEVELT, FORMER FIRST LADY

Since high school, I've skipped out on, oh, maybe twenty ski trips with my family and friends because I didn't know how to ski downhill. Well, I did try it once and was terrible at it, so I decided to get through life without again facing the embarrassment of skidding down the hill on my butt instead of on my skis.

Sounds stupid, right? I agree. I do take some solace in the fact that after all these years, I finally overcame my fear and went skiing, deciding to care more about learning how to do it than about how funny I look falling off the ski lift. I had an absolute blast, and while I was covered in snow and bruises by the end of my fall-filled day, I can now make it down a hill in one piece (as long as it's not a really steep hill, of course).

Dare to do something you don't think you're good at once in a while! You might try it and be even more awful than you thought you would be. So what? It's no fun being terrible at something and feeling like a fool, but missing out on fun, interesting, and possibly life-changing experiences is much more foolish. Even if you're not great at some activity, you might come to realize that you enjoy it and want to make it part of your life; sometimes you have to tell the perfectionist in you to take a break and have a blast! Of course, there's always the chance that you will attempt something and master it like a pro—think how hard you'll laugh at yourself for not having tried it sooner. No matter what, I can guarantee you this: If you dare yourself to conquer your fears about doing something you don't think you can, your life will be far from boring and dull. And what could be better than that?

Do you think that you can never learn to knit because the one time you tried, it was a disaster? Take a beginner's knitting class and see if you can conquer the world of yarn. Does roller-skating look like fun, but when you tried it earlier, you spent more time on the ground than on your feet? Find a friendly instructor, put on enough padding so that you can't see any part of your body, and give it a shot. Does yoga intrigue you, but you can hardly touch your toes and the last time you stretched was to reach for the remote? Grab a beginner's yoga video and try it out at home, without anyone watching, or check out a class (and stick to the back of the room). If you really want to, you *can* learn almost anything. The key is to:

1. Stop telling yourself that you can't do it.
2. Ignore what anyone else might think of what you're doing.
3. Imagine yourself becoming really good at what you're about to try.
4. Do it—just go, start, jump into it! The longer you wait, the more time you'll have to intimidate yourself, and that goes against point 1.

A friend of mine has always wanted to learn salsa dancing, but every time she was going to try it, she gave up at the last moment. It looked too difficult and complicated, and she didn't think that she could do it without making everyone around her laugh out loud. About a year ago she was changing jobs and found herself with a few free weeks on her hands. It was around the beginning of the year and she decided that rather than making yet another New Year's resolution about learning to salsa, she was just going to try it. She took a few classes, practiced on her own, and a few months later followed her passion all the way to Latin

America, where she spent weeks mastering the art of salsa—and falling in love with it—in the salsa capital of the world. It turned out that my friend had quite a knack for this beautiful dance and it's become one of her true passions in life. Even if she hadn't succeeded in mastering salsa dancing, finding the guts to try something she thought she could never do boosted her confidence and gave her the spirit to try a hundred other new things.

Have a sense of humor, allow yourself not to have to be great at everything you do, and life will be a whole lot more exciting!

DARING FEMALE I-MIGHT-NOT-BE-GREAT-AT-THIS-BUT-WANT-TO-TRY IDEAS

* Take a dance class that's way over your head.
* Write a poem, short story, or long story.
* Train for a 5K or a 10K or, hey, a marathon.
* Volunteer to lead a tough project at work.
* Sing karaoke—loudly, boldly, and with gusto.
* Make a cake from scratch—without a recipe.
* Speak up about your feelings and goals.
* Learn how to Rollerblade/ski/paint/knit/cook.
* Design and decorate a room in your apartment.

TAKE ON THE DARE

Write down a few things you will dare to try even though you might be absolutely awful at them or have no idea if you can ever pull them off.

_____

_____

_____

_____

_____

_____

Dare to Unclutter Your Life (at Least) Once a Year

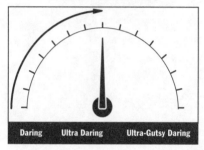

Through the years I've found it wonderful to acquire, but it is also wonderful to divest. It's rather like exhaling.

—HELEN HAYES, AMERICAN ACTRESS

Confession: I'm a bit of a neat freak. I like to have my stuff organized at home and at work, and although I haven't yet used a label maker to mark my spices and storage bins, I've definitely been tempted. Maybe it's inborn, but I also stay organized because I find that it lets me focus on what I really want to do and things I care about. Instead of having to spend an hour trying to find the latest draft of my book each time I want to work on it, I spend one hour organizing all of my files and then have the rest of my time to actually write my book.

In my quest to stay organized, clutter is one of my toughest enemies. We live in a small apartment and it doesn't take much for it to feel crowded. I always try to get rid of things we don't need and nag my husband to do the same. But things accumulate despite my efforts: magazines, newspapers, various tchotchkes, mementos from trips and birthdays—you know what I'm talking about. So a few times a year I spend a day uncluttering. I go through rooms, closets, and drawers and force myself to get rid of items if I don't see any use for them. It's not always easy: The funky-looking shirt I bought last year and wore exactly once still looks really fun, but will I ever wear it again? If the answer involves any hesitation on my part, away that particular item goes (if possible, to a thrift store). Uncluttering our apartment makes me feel refreshed, cleansed, and peaceful.

A while back I realized that while I'm pretty good about getting rid of physical clutter, I often ignore the emotional or mental clutter that just sits there and weighs me down. I might have a few tense phone conversations with a friend and then let the negativity brew instead of doing something about it. Or I'll keep fretting about something for months without a resolution and without doing anything to stem my worries. This emotional clutter (baggage, weight, burden, or whatever else you want to call it) is much harder to clear out than throwing out a few pairs of old shoes. I try not to chicken out of dealing with it, and although I can't claim anything close to 100 percent success, it helps me live my life with a clearer and more energized mind.

Dare to unclutter your life (at least) once a year! Set aside a few hours and psych yourself up to deal with every piece of clutter you can find. You'll feel refreshed, organized, cleansed, and in control of your life rather than trapped by it. I promise.

As the first step, unclutter your living and working space. Go through your closets, drawers, bins, and storage containers and get rid of anything if it fits any of the following criteria:

- You have no idea what the particular object is or what it does.
- You don't remember the last time you used it/wore it/ looked at it.
- You try hard to think of when you'll use it/wear it/look at it, but you can't.
- You have more than one but can only ever recall using/ wearing one.

Be relentless and tough. Clutter can try to trick you by appealing to your sentimental or nostalgic feelings: for example, "I don't ever wear these hideous earrings, but I bought them the same year I met my husband." Sure, some things are dear to your heart and you'll want to keep them forever. Just don't apply that definition too broadly. You'll also find it useful to organize the things you decide to keep. Filing cabinets are great for storing loose papers, receipts, past tax returns, and so on. If you really must keep every one of your old photos but don't want the hassle of organizing them in photo albums, run out to your local craft or office supply store and buy a few small storage boxes where you can keep them neatly. Label each folder in the filing cabinet and each box so that you know what it contains. These steps might seem trivial, but trust me, seeing a pile of labeled boxes instead of many disorganized piles of random photos can do wonders for your peace of mind.

Ahhhh! Now that you've uncluttered your physical space, time for the second step: getting rid of your mental clutter. Grab a cup of something you like to drink, sit down, and think about what's been weighing you down. The more honest you are with yourself, the more clutter you'll clear from your mind. I suggest making a quick list—writing things down makes it hard to continue avoiding them. Then set a short period of time during which you'll try to take care of each item on your list. "Next Tuesday I'll call my sister and make up after that terrible fight we had" is better than "At some point I have to call my sister." Stick to your list and time line, and as you get rid of each piece of mental clutter, cross it off. You'll feel an incredible mix of relief and energy, and free your mind to focus on more positive, productive, and fun things. Take my word for it: The benefits will be endless!

DARING FEMALE UNCLUTTER CHECKLIST

PHYSICAL CLUTTER

- Old magazines, books, newspapers, receipts, theater programs, menus

- Old clothes, jewelry, coats, shoes

- Random objects, mementos, souvenirs

- Useless dishes, spices, foods you don't recognize

EMOTIONAL CLUTTER

- Things you're endlessly worrying about

- Conflicts you need to resolve

- Life decisions you need to make

- Plans you need to finalize

TAKE ON THE DARE

Look at a calendar. Pick a date for your first life uncluttering day. Write it down. Stick to it. When it comes, create a list of emotional and material clutter you want to expunge from your life and dare yourself to go for it with full force!

_____

_____

_____

_____

_____

_____

Dare to Get on the Train First and Then Worry About Where It's Going

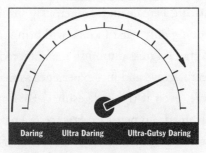

DARE-METER

Daring   Ultra Daring   Ultra-Gutsy Daring

One of my strengths is following my life when it takes a turn. I think you have to be open to a happy accident.

—SUSAN SARANDON, AMERICAN ACTRESS

I used to think that life would be great if somehow I could see into the future and know where each step I'm taking is going to lead. For example, if I take this job today, then in two years I'll be promoted; in five years I'll be a really big honcho; and in ten years I will finally have a job I love, with tons of responsibility, flexibility, interesting work, and oh yes, a nice paycheck.

Or if I take this job today I'll end up in a dead-end situation, with an unsupportive boss and no opportunities for advancement.

Either way, I'd know whether each opportunity was worth pursuing and wouldn't waste my time on situations that weren't going to have a great outcome.

I feel lucky that this magic window through which I could see my life five years from now doesn't exist (and if it does, don't tell me where to find it). I couldn't think of a more non–Daring Female and dangerously limiting way to live than by doing only what I know will bring me a specific desired outcome. I'd miss out on so many incredible opportunities to learn, grow, and just experience as many facets of life as possible, even if the end result is far from what I'd wanted or dreamed. I'd never experience the pride of working hard for something I really want, even if my efforts don't bring the desired outcome. And I'd never discover things about myself that we get to learn only when we face difficulties, unpredictable situations, or failure. Just the thought of living a safe and unfulfilling life like that gives me the creeps.

Dare to get on the train first and then worry about where it's going! When you're presented with an opportunity, don't spend time overanalyzing where it will take you every step of the way and how it will ultimately work out. If you know the general direction you're headed in and that's the way you'd like to go, take a deep, daring breath and hit the road. You may find that your path is everything you expected, and perhaps more. Or you may discover that it's leading you in an unintended direction, and then you have a chance to decide what to do: Go there anyway and explore something new or return to where you started. Either way, you can use what you've learned to guide your life to a place where you'd really like to be. Don't limit your life and deny yourself wonderful surprises and unexpected benefits by always having to know exactly what impact something you do today will have on your life tomorrow. If you never do something without being sure of the final outcome, then you risk doing not much of anything at all.

Say you decide to take a new job in an industry you don't know very much about and in a position that's not exactly what you wanted. You're a Daring Female and you know that life is way too short to wait around for the perfect opportunity to come your way; most of the time you have to take an imperfect opportunity, roll up your sleeves, and mold it into something you truly love and want. So you take the job and a year later realize that this industry is much more intriguing than you ever imagined. You work hard and get promoted, finding yourself in a position far more interesting and rewarding than one you could ever have pictured for yourself. Or maybe the complete opposite happens: You end up hating the industry and your job, but in the process learn about ten other things you'd much rather do. You start a fresh job search, armed with more knowledge about yourself and what you'd like to do in your next gig. After you get a job you really like, you can appreciate what your bad job experience has taught you. Either way, you're a gutsy Daring Female, living your life, taking chances, and using your power to gain something from every opportunity and make your life more interesting, ecstatic, and filled with unique experiences you wouldn't give up in a million years.

Alex Ramsey is a Daring Female who has never let a lack of experience or the unpredictability of events prevent her from taking on intriguing opportunities. A food lover, she decided to start her own restaurant when she was young, inexperienced, and pregnant. Opening a restaurant was something she'd wanted to do for a while, but she had no idea how difficult it would be: A week after her baby was born, she found herself in the kitchen, cooking the meals herself while her baby lay near her on a blanket, because her two chefs had suddenly walked out. Many sleep-deprived months and bank troubles later, Alex decided to sell her restaurant; this train wasn't going where she wanted to go. A few months after this, Alex's friend approached her with an unexpected offer: to write a gossip column for her city's newspaper. Without much writing experience and with little idea of what this job would be like, Alex accepted. She needed a complete change of pace and the job sounded like it would be fun for a short while. Alex stayed for four years, learning a whole new craft and getting a chance to interview everyone from Liza Minnelli to Bruce Springsteen.

Eventually, after many great experiences, Alex began to feel like she was stuck and wanted to do something more meaningful with her life. Another friend of hers had just moved nearby and wanted to start a business teaching people how to apply theater skills to improve their business communication skills. She asked Alex to join her in starting a company, which they did, on Alex's dinner table. The company grew quickly, teaching Alex not only about starting her own business but about the power of strong interpersonal communication. It was those skills that Alex used twelve years later, when she started her very own management consulting company, which she still runs today.

Not every opportunity Alex pursued in her life turned out the way she thought it would or the way she wanted. But each experience was rewarding in its own way, filled with invaluable lessons, and each made it possible for her to figure out that what she really wanted to do with her life was run her own business, one that helped people and companies become more successful and better at what they do.

There's no way to know where you'll end up every time you take on a new challenge or pursue a new opportunity. And that's the absolutely great thing about living a Daring Female life! It allows you to be surprised, to experience success as well as failure, and to learn something from each situation that guides your future choices and brings you closer to filling your life with things you care about and want to be doing. Dare yourself to take on opportunities that come your way and stop worrying about how each will turn out. Have confidence in yourself and top it off with a healthy dose of faith. You're a gutsy Daring Female and you'll find a way to use every chance you get to make your life more fulfilling and exciting.

DARING FEMALE REASONS TO HOP ON THE TRAIN

- It looks intriguing.
- It's going in the general direction you'd like to go.
- You've never taken this particular train before.
- It's filled with interesting and dynamic people you'd love to meet.
- It might be the very last train.
- You can't just stand there, so you might as well go somewhere.
- Why *not* get on this train?

TAKE ON THE DARE

Write down a couple of opportunities you're facing and dare to roll up your sleeves and take one on, even if it isn't exactly what you want or you don't know exactly how it will work out.

_____

_____

_____

_____

_____

_____

Dare to Live It, Not Count It

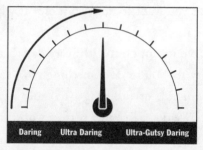

You don't get to choose how you're going to die. Or when.
You can only decide how you're going to live. Now.
— JOAN BAEZ, AMERICAN FOLKSINGER

I think that knowing how to count isn't always a good thing. Sometimes it can drive us all a bit nuts. Just think about the number of articles you read every day that tell you how you should dress in your twenties, what you should eat in your thirties, and where you should be in your career and your savings account by the time you're forty. I'm all for good advice, but advice like this can lead us to an unnecessary and limiting obsession with age and where we should be at certain times in our lives.

Who cares how old you are when you reach a peak in your career? Or if you refuse to change how you dress just because you're celebrating another birthday? The fact that most women your age—or most of your friends or your friends' friends—do things in a certain way doesn't mean for a second that you necessarily should, too. High school is behind you; the pressure to fit in with your classmates should stay back there with it. This is your life and you get to decide what you want to do with it and at what age you feel like doing it.

Dare to live it, not count it! Every day that goes by is an opportunity for you to do something new, exciting, enjoyable, meaningful, or fulfilling—to truly live it in the way *you* want. We don't live in a perfect world and we have to find a way to realize our goals amid endless obstacles and constraints. Dare yourself not to let your age become one of those obstacles. You might want to do something but then think "I'm too young for this" or "I'm too old for this." If thoughts like this sneak into your head, kick them out and ask yourself this question: "Too young or old compared to whom?" Some national statistical average? Social norms? Your friends' opinions about what people should do with their lives at a certain age? None of these seem as relevant or important as what you want to do at whatever age you want to do it.

While working on this book, I came across the story of Emily Kimball, who is an amazing example of how great life can be when you focus on living it in whatever way suits you, regardless of how old you are. At the age of sixty, Emily did something that I bet many people would think was more appropriate for a thirty-year-old: She set out to hike the entire Appalachian Trail from Georgia to Maine, all 2,168 miles of it. Having to overcome everything from a stress fracture to snowstorms and lightning strikes, Emily conquered what I think is an even tougher obstacle: thinking she was too old to attempt this great adventure. She managed to get through the grueling hike with flying colors by being flexible (completing parts of the hike one month each year instead of all at once), focusing on her love for physical activity and the outdoors, and doing an enormous amount of research and preparation before she began. As I learned about Emily's story, I could feel her excitement and pride when she reached her goal of climbing to the top of Mount Katahdin at the end of her nine-year journey. She was literally on top of the world! And I am pretty sure that the last thing she worried about as she stood there was how old she was or why it took her nine years to make one of her life dreams come true. (Emily has taken seriously her life mantra to do what you want when you want, regardless of your age or how hard it may seem. She now shares her message with the rest of the world through her Web site, www.theagingadventurer .com, and her energizing talks.)

If you want to experience and do things but feel constrained by thoughts of being too young or too old, try this: Once in a blue moon do something small that you think is completely out of character for someone your age. Go to a concert where the audience will probably be much younger than you, check out a gallery opening that you think will mostly attract an older sophisticated crowd, or go shopping in a store you haven't set foot in since you were much younger. Break your perceived age boundaries in small ways and see what happens. I guarantee one of two things will happen: No one will care about what you've done or people will respect you for doing something different. I started off this chapter by saying you shouldn't care about what others think, and I stand by that as one of the most essential Daring Female mantras. I realize that what others think often influences us and is the source of many opinions and notions we form about ourselves and the world. So go for it—take your notions for a ride by testing them out in small ways you can handle. And when you see that the world doesn't come to an end just because you don't act your age, take that reality and use it to free your mind from whatever age-related constraints it might hold. Just think of all the great things you could be doing with the time you spend worrying about being too young or too old, and go out and do them! I guarantee that many pleasant surprises are waiting for you!

DARING FEMALE WAYS TO FAIL MATH

* Do something every week that you haven't done in ten years but that makes your mouth stretch into a wide smile: Indulge in a banana split, dance around your house to your favorite music, or run through sprinklers in the summer.
* Organize a "Don't Act Your Age" day and spend it with your most Daring Female friends, doing things that no respectable women of your age would consider doing.
* The next time you're asked about your age, make your answer your favorite age—one you've been, you are, or you will be in the future.
* Write out five things that you don't think people your age do/should do and do each once, or twice if you dare.
* Instead of celebrating your birthday every year, pick a random date and celebrate your nonbirthday. Make each one a special occasion that celebrates an achievement or success you care about.

TAKE ON THE DARE

Write down three things that you're going to do for which you might think you're too old or too young. Dare to do at least one in the next week.

_____

_____

_____

_____

_____

_____

Dare to Dedicate Six Weeks a Year to Forming a New Habit (or Kicking One You Can't Stand)

DARE-METER

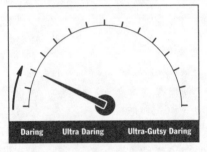

A finished person is a boring person.

—ANNA QUINDLEN, AMERICAN WRITER

My mom, who is a piano teacher, tells me that I have great pitch. She's heard me hum songs around the house, and when I let it all hang out at my bachelorette karaoke party, she was impressed. But my perfect pitch has not always made me a great listener. When my mind is racing at a hundred miles an hour (which is often), I sometimes find myself interrupting people or thinking about something else if I already know the point they are making. I am a generally friendly and sensitive person, so a few years back, I decided that I needed to get in the habit of being a better listener.

Right about that same time I heard a piece on the radio in which it was mentioned that it usually takes six weeks to form a habit. Perfect—I was going to spend the next six weeks giving my listening skills a much-needed tune-up. I made up my mind that during this time I was not going to interrupt anyone for any reason, and I stuck to it. I remember standing at the car rental counter on one of my trips for work and listening for what seemed like an eternity as the agent described all the possible insurance options I could choose. I traveled a lot and knew these by heart, but a promise is a promise: I was not going to interrupt him. I bit my tongue and listened, a technique I found worked really well to prevent me from jumping in before the other person was finished. During my six weeks of forming the habit of being a good listener I also made a conscious effort to focus on what I was hearing and not think of anything else during that time—no going over my to-do lists or thinking of how I was going to approach a project at work. When I listened, I was 100 percent there.

I didn't have a scientific way to measure my progress, but I felt that after six weeks I was a better listener, someone with whom people wanted to share their thoughts and news, and someone who made them feel good while they were doing it. I still have a big mouth and like to talk, but because I am able to listen better, the people with whom I talk also feel great about talking to me. And I know that this makes me a better friend, colleague, and rental car customer.

Dare to dedicate six weeks a year to forming a new habit! It can be anything—drinking more water, reading the newspaper every day, being the first to speak up in meetings, fitting some type of heart-pumping activity into every day, or anything else. All of us can use a few more good habits in our lives. So pick one and dare yourself to spend the next six weeks making your life that much better.

Or maybe you have a habit you really can't stand (c'mon, who doesn't?) and you'd like to boot it out of your life. Pick a date, get psyched up, and spend the next six weeks getting rid of it. I don't think there's anything magical about six weeks, but it's a good chunk of time to spend focused on changing your life in a small or perhaps not so small way. A six-week period is not so short that your habit-forming actions won't have a chance to find a somewhat permanent place in your life, and it's not so long as to be intimidating when you start.

Before you start your six-week quest, take some time and write down a few specific steps you'll take each day to reinforce your new habit or rid yourself of your old one. The more specific you can be, the better. That way, instead of having to think about it you'll have your daily action list to follow and stick to. Say you decide to get in the habit of going to the gym more often. Here are a few action steps that you could include on your list:

- Lay out my gym clothes on the couch before I leave for work.
- As soon as I come home, change into my gym clothes and put my workout sneakers by the door.
- Go to the gym every Monday and Thursday from 7:00 P.M. until 8:00 P.M., and on Saturday from 11:00 A.M. until noon, regardless of the weather or how busy or tired I am.
- On these days, put "Go to the gym" on my to-do list and on the home/family calendar.
- At the gym, ask for help in creating a workout routine that I can easily follow on my own.

These are just a few ideas to get you thinking in the right direction—the more specific you are, the more effective your six weeks will be. The habit you're trying to form or kick might seem trivial, but the smallest changes that improve your life can make a huge difference. I've found that it's harder to go out there, conquer the world, and get every ounce of enjoyment out of life if an annoying habit is nagging me or if I know that I should be doing something (such as drinking more water) that I'm not. Try it and see for yourself!

A FEW DARING FEMALE FAVORITE HABITS

- Express myself when I have something to say and make sure to let others do the same.

- Give my body a daily zoom of energy: Walk, run, climb stairs, jump rope, work out, anything to get the blood flowing!

- Do something good for the world as often as possible: Recycle, vote, donate old clothes instead of throwing them out.

- Finish what I start even if I get bored, tired, or annoyed.

- Don't rely on things like cigarettes, food, alcohol, or coffee to make myself feel better. Instead, deal with the actual problem that's causing me to feel down.

- Make someone smile or laugh once a day.

- Be early.

- Remember friends' birthdays and surprise them with funky handmade cards.

TAKE ON THE DARE

Write down three habits you want to form or kick and dare to dedicate six weeks this year to making one of them happen.

_____

_____

_____

_____

_____

_____

Laugh
a Little,
Live a Lot

DF A Daring Female isn't a Daring Female if she can't laugh her heart out or have outrageous amounts of fun once in a while. And she isn't true to her Daring Female self if she doesn't rely on her sense of humor to get her out of tough or embarrassing situations. Life gives us way too many reasons to be upset, get sad, or walk around feeling gray and unhappy. It's up to us to find reasons not to feel that way as often as humanly possible. So don't hesitate—crack a smile for absolutely no other reason than it's better to smile than not. And read on for some inspiration to spend more of your days feeling like you have a lot to smile about.

Dare to Have Outrageous Amounts of Fun

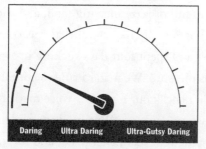

DARE-METER

Daring   Ultra Daring   Ultra-Gutsy Daring

Life seems to love the liver of it.

—MAYA ANGELOU, AMERICAN POET AND NOVELIST

When was the last time you had so much fun that all of your worries, regrets, and to-do lists were far from your mind and the only thing you could do was enjoy the moment? Sure, we all do something we like from time to time: read a book, go to a movie, spend time with our partners or kids or pets. But once in a while we have to completely break out of our routine and find ways to enjoy life to the fullest. We have to have an "Ahhh! I feel so good!" moment.

I realized how important this was a few years ago. My husband and I had been working around the clock for months; we were mentally and physically exhausted and started to feel as if we were literally out of breath. We'd take a night off here or there and get some takeout or go to a movie, but it seemed as if it had been ages since we did something we absolutely loved. So we decided to take a short trip to New Orleans, a city we had never visited but had heard was full of jazz, amazing food, and happy people. We splurged on a really nice hotel that was completely out of our budget and spent four days sucking in every ounce of New Orleans pleasure. We made a rule to not talk about our jobs and didn't check our e-mail or voice mail at home. Our trip was only four days long, but it felt much longer and we came back home refreshed, energized, and full of memories of a vacation we'd never forget.

Dare yourself to have outrageous amounts of fun once in a while! Maybe you've been working crazy hours and need an energizing break. Or you feel like you've been stuck in an endless routine. If you feel like you need to infuse your life with fun, do it. Just make sure to really go for it and plan an activity that's outrageously fun and really exciting. Go to a restaurant you've been fantasizing about but can't normally afford, plan a weekend getaway to a cozy bed-and-breakfast, or spend a day at an amusement park without your kids. If you get butterflies in your stomach and a big grin on your face thinking about it, you know you're on the right track to planning your outrageously fun activity.

You wouldn't think that you need to remind yourself to have fun, but you do. The hectic lives many of us lead make it too easy to forget that sometimes we need to take a deep breath, forget our stress, worries, and responsibilities, and do something wonderfully enjoyable. I bet you can come up with many great excuses for why you just can't manage a few outrageously fun hours (or dare I say days) right now: You can't afford it, you're too busy at home with your kids or too stressed about a project at work, or you just don't feel up to it. But I dare you to find a way to counter any excuse and zap yourself with a much-needed fun-filled break. If you're creative about it, outrageous fun doesn't have to cost much. You can find a family member, friend, or neighbor who will watch your kids for a short while. Your project at work will welcome your refreshed attitude and energized mind when you come back. Not feeling up to an adventure is precisely why you should plan a few hours of fun immediately!

So how about it?

DARING FEMALE OUTRAGEOUS FUN IDEAS

· **Plan a Daring Female scavenger hunt for your favorite fun-loving friends.**
Divide the group into two. Pick a bunch of places around where you live and
assign to each a crazy, funky, outrageous activity that each group must
perform there. Use your imagination! How about making pizza at the local
pizza parlor? Performing as street musicians? Strutting down the town's
main street as drag queens? Each group should have a disposable camera
so they can take pictures of themselves performing each activity as proof of
their daring completion of the scavenger hunt. After everyone is done, get
the pictures developed and spend a few laughter-filled hours looking
through them, arguing about whose feat was the most daring.

· **Get away for a weekend with your favorite person in the world.** Go to a
bed-and-breakfast that's out of your budget or take a last-minute trip
somewhere warm (if it's cold) or somewhere cold (if it's warm). Site59.com
is a great Web site with tons of affordable last-minute getaway deals, so be
resourceful and have a weekend you won't forget.

· **Spend an entire day doing only things that you always wished you could
but rarely do.** Maybe you've always wanted to play tourist in your own city.
Or you've been eyeing the new ice rink but haven't found the time to
practice your swirls. Or perhaps you've been dreaming of spending an entire
day completely disconnected from the world—no phone, no TV, no computer,
just you and whatever tickles your soul. This is your day to do it!

· **Take your physical endurance for a ride.** Fill a day or a weekend with your
favorite outdoor activities; make sure to fit in at least one that you've never
tried. Take a four-hour hike, go rock climbing or white-water rafting, learn
how to snowboard or ski or skillfully navigate a mountain in a snow tire. Let
your brain chill out from the daily grind and give your other muscles
something to conquer.

TAKE ON THE DARE

Write down a few things you'd like to do for your outrageous fun moments and dare to do at least one in the next month.

_____

_____

_____

_____

_____

_____

Dare to Laugh at Yourself

DARE-METER

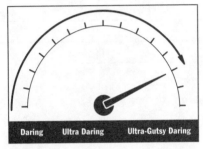

*The one important thing I've learned over the years is the
difference between taking one's work seriously and
taking oneself seriously. The first is imperative
and the second is disastrous.*

—MARGOT FONTEYN, BRITISH BALLET DANCER

I don't like to brag, but I've been laughed at a *lot* in my
life. Most of this laughter came from my kind high
school classmates, who couldn't get enough of my funny
English, strange clothes, and awkward behavior once I
joined their ranks after immigrating from Russia to the
United States. I've since learned from my American friends

that you don't need to mispronounce words or eat hot dogs on flat bread instead of hot dog buns (who knew?) to get laughed at during high school, but I can tell you that it definitely helps.

Being laughed at was no fun. It made me miserable and incredibly insecure. I'm anything but shy or quiet, but I spoke little during my first couple of years in America out of fear of saying something wrong and being laughed at. I remember being called on once to read a passage in history class; I tried to control my nerves and seemingly got through it without a major faux pas. But as I read the last word, the room swelled up with a collective giggle as my teacher kindly pointed out that *herbs* was pronounced without the *h*. Duh.

What made it all worse was the fact that there was another immigrant in my class, a girl, whose English was worse than mine, who brought really bizarre food for lunch, but who somehow avoided being a source of constant entertainment for our classmates. I couldn't figure out how she did it and was burning up with envy until we ended up at the same lunch table one day. After a few minutes around her, I figured out her secret: Instead of letting other students laugh at her, she laughed at herself first! She'd say something incorrectly, realize it, and then boom, just break into laughter. "Wow, that came out weird," she'd say with a smile, and to my utter shock, instead of laughing at her, our tablemates would just wave it off and say something like "Hey, who cares? Don't worry about it."

I was impressed. Although it took a while to muster up the guts to do it, I decided that I was going to become an expert at self-laughter. I'd be the first to acknowledge when I mispronounced something in English or when my mom made me something funny-looking for lunch, and I'd do it with a smile and a giggle. And when I had no clue who some famous TV personality was, I'd be the first to laugh at my own ignorance. Was this easy to do? Definitely not. Did it work? Not all the time, but as I learned to laugh at myself, it changed my life. I stopped being afraid of making a silly mistake or of seeming stupid and just thought about all those things as small mishaps, nothing I couldn't get over with a few laughs. Because I was more at ease with myself, my classmates felt more relaxed around me, and when I did hear their laughter at something I said or did, it was usually together with my own and had a new, kinder ring to it. I couldn't believe it, but I even started to feel quite cool about being able to make everyone laugh.

Even though I now speak English without an accent and have an extensive knowledge of American pop-culture icons, I try never to pass up an opportunity to laugh at myself. Whether I'm laughing at one of my weird habits or an awkward situation I've just created, I connect with people around me and open up to them by showing that I'm human, I do silly things, and just like them, I find those things pretty funny. In fact, being able to laugh at your mistakes often brings more respect from others than always being right and put together.

Dare to laugh at yourself! It might not feel natural, but the next time you make a silly mistake or embarrass yourself, try to be the first to laugh about it. Start small: Do this first in a safe place, while you're with people you trust and feel comfortable around. Then try it outside of your immediate comfort zone—say, at work, on a date, or at a party. You don't need to break out into full-blown make-your-stomach-hurt laughter, but be genuine about it. With time, you might find that laughing at yourself comes naturally and you even like doing it. It can make you feel much less uptight about life, which is incredibly liberating.

Being able to laugh at the silly, embarrassing, and quirky things you do might not seem like a great achievement, but it makes a huge difference. It has the power to make you more confident, more open to new situations and opportunities, more willing to take on risks. If you know that making a mistake in front of dozens of people isn't the end of the world, and better, if you can laugh about it, then you'll always have the confidence to just be yourself and the guts to do what you want. And hey, if that's not the essence of being a Daring Female, I can't imagine what is!

HOLLYWOOD DARING FEMALES WHO DON'T TAKE THEMSELVES TOO SERIOUSLY

DARING FEMALE	CHECK HER OUT IN . . .
• Diane Keaton	*Annie Hall*
• Rosie O'Donnell	*A League of Their Own*
• Reese Witherspoon	*Legally Blonde*
• Janeane Garofalo	*The Truth About Cats and Dogs*
• Nia Vardalos	*My Big Fat Greek Wedding*
• Drew Barrymore	*The Wedding Singer*
• Lili Taylor	*Mystic Pizza*
• Marisa Tomei	*My Cousin Vinny*
• Joan Cusack	*Nine Months*

TAKE ON THE DARE

Write down a few funny qualities you have or embarrassing life experiences you can now laugh about—or at least would like to. And dare to be the first to laugh at yourself the next chance you get.

_____

_____

_____

_____

_____

_____

Dare to Color Outside the Lines

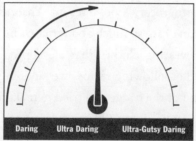

DARE-METER

| Daring | Ultra Daring | Ultra-Gutsy Daring |

If you obey all the rules you miss all the fun.
—KATHARINE HEPBURN, AMERICAN ACTRESS

Not everything we learn in kindergarten is good for us. Sharing toys and cookies, not pushing each other on the playground, saying thank you—sure, these are important life skills. But staying inside the lines when we color, wearing matching socks, and lining up in a straight line outside the classroom are things I think many of us learn a little too well. Just look around your world: Isn't it a little too perfect, too organized, too full of straight lines and matching everything? We drive in straight lanes of traffic, stand in organized lines at the store, wear shirts that match our pants, type spell-checked documents and e-mails, cook according to recipes, and follow a bunch of other rules and conventions without thinking about them twice.

Wouldn't life be much more fun if from time to time we forgot some of our kindergarten education? No, I'm definitely not suggesting that we drive on the wrong side of the road or turn grocery-store lines into chaotic messes, but what if we didn't care so much about matching our socks to our pants or wearing clothes that are appropriate for our age? If instead of following recipes we randomly picked ten ingredients out of the fridge and tried to make a meal out of them? If we drank juice out of wineglasses and wine out of juice glasses? Wouldn't our lives swell up with more color and laughter? I scream a resounding yes!

Dare to color outside the lines! Whether you're an ultraorganized and serious adult or someone who lets her hair down and dances around the house to unbearably loud music from time to time, all of us can use more "Who cares about the rules?" moments in our lives. The routines that we follow day after day are necessary for all of us to survive in this crowded, complicated world, but they can make us feel stiff, constrained, and dull. The great news is that we can and absolutely positively should take frequent breaks from our serious adult lives. In fact, I don't think this is an option: If you want to maintain your sanity and live a full, fun life, you *have* to do it.

I have a friend who, probably without knowing it, always reminds me to take breaks from being a well-behaved serious adult. Every time we meet up for a quick drink after work (which due to our hectic adult lives isn't as often as I'd like), her hair is a different color and styled in a cool, funky way I don't dare risk with my own hair. Although she has a serious adult job she's always wearing something fun and different, something I bet I couldn't find in any store whose name I can spell. She's always telling me about a recipe she made up and wants to know what new stuff I've been cooking. She is a breath of fresh air every time I see her and a poster child of a Daring Female for whom coloring outside the lines comes more naturally than staying inside them.

Escaping from your serious adult mode, acting a bit, or a lot, out of your norm from time to time isn't difficult, but it has some pretty wonderful effects. It helps you feel more free and unrestricted in your life. It reminds you that following rules is just one way to live and encourages you to explore other ways of looking at things. Most of all, allowing yourself the freedom to forget your adult ways helps you feel more alive. Try it and see how amazing it can be!

DARING FEMALE IDEAS FOR COLORING
OUTSIDE THE LINES

We all need inspiration to be a little less adult in our lives, so here are a few ideas to get your not-so-serious juices flowing:

* For a week, wear one thing every day that doesn't go with the rest of your outfit—a funky scarf, wild socks, a brightly colored bag, or a shirt that makes that annoying person in your office who always comments on people's clothes say, "Where in the world did you get that?"
* Have an "opposites" food day: Eat breakfast food for dinner, dinner food for breakfast, and your favorite dessert for lunch.
* Reshuffle your alphabetized CD collection and organize it by mood.
* Paint a wall or several walls in your house in bright, bold colors that don't quite go with your home's personality.
* For your next get-together, forget fancy china, traditional table settings, or adult food. Instead, set up a picnic on the floor and serve fun food that's easy to eat without utensils.

TAKE ON THE DARE

Write down three things you're going to do this week to
take a break from your serious adult life and dare to have
some fun with them.

_____

_____

_____

_____

_____

_____

Dare to Just Get in a Good Mood

DARE-METER

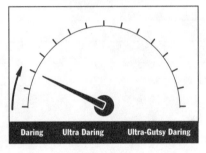

He who laughs, lasts.

—MARY PETTIBONE POOLE, WRITER

If you've lived through the eighties, then you probably know the movie *Say Anything*, with John Cusack and Ione Skye (or perhaps you remember them as Lloyd Dobler and Diane Court). I didn't get to see this movie until a few years ago, when my husband decided that my life would never be truly fulfilling if I didn't see all of the great American movies I missed while growing up abroad. *Say Anything* was one of many on his list. It's a quirky, lighthearted comedy that wouldn't have had much impact on me except for one scene. In it, Lloyd Dobler is talking to his sister (who happens to be Joan Cusack, his sister in real life). She is cranky and seemingly unhappy, in no small part due to the fact that her boyfriend or husband (we don't know which) has recently left her and her young son. Lloyd, who is an eternal optimist and someone who sees life through slightly pinkish, if not completely rosy, sunglasses, looks at her and says, "Why can't you just get in a good mood once in a while?"

A few weeks after we saw the movie I had one of those "I'm feeling blue but I'm not sure why" days. You know, those days when nothing makes you smile, when stuff you don't usually mind annoys the heck out of you, when you feel like staying in bed all day with the shades down. The only moderately positive emotion I could muster came from knowing that this day was close to being over. As I walked home from work that day, the line from the movie popped into my head and got me thinking: Why couldn't I just get into a good mood? There was nothing specific that I could blame for making me cranky and unhappy, so why did I feel that way?

I'm no happy-go-lucky person, but generally being in a good mood just feels so much better than the opposite, and it helps me live my life in a fuller, more exciting, and fulfilling way. (And I'm certainly much more pleasant to be around—just ask my husband!) So I decided to try it: to get in a good mood (okay, maybe a decent mood to start with) without any specific reason or occasion. After all, I was walking in one of my favorite cities in the whole wide world, I was in good health and so was most of my family, I had a job I didn't hate and a husband I loved, and most of the time I was managing to find enough time to follow my passion for writing. Not too shabby, and definitely enough to make me feel better than okay even on the bluest of days. I can't tell you that I suddenly felt on top of the world, but thinking about these wonderful things in my life that I usually take for granted did start to make me feel less cranky.

Dare to just get in a good mood! You don't have to run around every day with a huge smile on your face. All of us have different personalities, and some might find it easier than others to move through life with an upbeat attitude. But you've got to agree that feeling up is much better than feeling down. When we feel good, we're full of hope and confidence; we give off positive vibes that make it so much easier to get as much great stuff out of our lives as humanly possible.

The best thing about getting in a good mood is that you don't really need a special reason to feel upbeat and positive. Sure, getting a surprise bouquet of flowers, acing a tough project at work, getting a huge hug from your boyfriend/husband/kids, or seeing a great comedy at the movie theater can help. But think about this: Aren't being alive, breathing, seeing, feeling, and walking around pretty powerful reasons to get in a good mood? Without a doubt, although I bet that we sometimes take these things for granted. Break the habit and don't take them for granted!

Smile because you're healthy, feel happy because you woke up today, and get in a good mood because life is better that way. If you have days when you're blue, then you should definitely have days when you're the brightest kind of sunshine-yellow. And if you need to give yourself a little push to get there, do it! Recognize your Daring Female power to control your moods and use it to feel as positive and optimistic as possible. Be that person who stands out from the rush-hour crowd of sullen faces with a smile or a sparkle in her eye or a slight lift to her step. Make people wonder what you're so happy about, and revel in the knowledge that you're feeling good just because you're living your life, with no specific reason in sight. Try it and see how great it feels!

Life is way too short to spend it feeling bad about yourself or unhappy. And unfortunately, it is filled with terrible events that have every right in the world to make us genuinely sad. We have to cherish the days when things are okay and make the most of them by getting in a good mood and using it as fuel to live with more energy and oomph in our every step.

DARING FEMALE GOOD MOOD INSPIRATIONS

- You woke up this morning.

- When you want to take a breath there's always enough air for you to do it.

- Everything changes: If you hate today's weather or have a bad day at work, tomorrow it could all be different.

- There are people in your life who love you, and there are people whom you love.

- Being in a good mood feels better than being in a terrible mood.

- You're a free person and can do anything you want with your life (even if you can't do it right now or you don't know exactly what you want).

TAKE ON THE DARE

Jot down a few thoughts or revelations that make you feel good about your life. Dare to remember them when you're feeling blue and use them to propel yourself into a better, more positive mood.

_____

_____

_____

_____

_____

Dare to Share Your Special Vibes with the World

DARE-METER

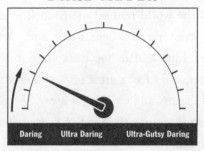

Daring   *Ultra Daring*   *Ultra-Gutsy Daring*

*Let's dare to be ourselves for we do that
better than anyone else.*

—SHIRLEY BRIGGS, AMERICAN WILDLIFE ARTIST

There are some people in the world who seem to just beam positive energy. When you're around them, their energy makes you feel really great, even if you're having the worst possible day. It's almost addictive to be with people like that, but it's the most wonderful kind of addiction, and definitely one you don't want to kick.

I recently met a woman whose positive energy immediately drew me from across the room—literally. From the first conversation we ever had, I knew that this was someone I'd love to have in my life. This might not sound so odd except that our conversation had to do with the financial service industry (in which both of us spend our working days), definitely not a subject that usually makes me grin. But this amazing energy always comes from her regardless of what we talk about. She focuses on the positive side of even the toughest situations, and her optimism and unwillingness to get down on the world remind me to look at my own life through the most positive lens I can find. After I spend time with her, I get a little hop in my step, my heart beats just a bit faster, and I feel a great urge to do something fun, creative, and daring, and do it right away. She fills me with a buzz of energy, and it's the kind of energy of which I can never get enough.

Dare to share your special vibes with the world! All of us have our own ways of making those around us feel better, more energized, more hopeful, more creative, more powerful, more confident. Maybe you're the Daring Female version of the infamous Energizer Bunny, always going a hundred miles a minute and doing more in a day than most of us do in a week. Realize how unusual that is and how much your energy can help others who may not have the same drive and energy. Maybe you're super confident and have an effective high kick against intimidation and self-doubt. Or perhaps you're someone with a quirky and ever-present sense of humor, who makes people laugh without even trying to do it. Whatever your special sauce, realize how awesome it is, and don't be shy or greedy about sharing it with the people around you. Let your never-ending energy spill out, practice your anti-intimidation high kick in public, or make jokes and act silly until people laugh so hard that their stomachs hurt. You never know exactly how your special vibes affect those around you, but you can count on the fact that they do make a difference in someone's life.

I know you wouldn't dare to do this, but I can hear some of you suggest that you may not have any special sauce the rest of the world might want to taste. If you even start to think in that direction, stop immediately. No two people in the world are alike, and you have more wonderful qualities than you realize. You may feel strange showing them off, but you shouldn't. Someone out there needs your humor to make her day go smoother or your confidence to inspire her own or your energy to keep working at a task that doesn't ever seem to get done. You may not know if you've inspired someone or given someone confidence or peace of mind, but if you let yourself be yourself and feel free to spread your own special vibes around you, more people will benefit than you can ever imagine.

Being yourself is a start, but you can take your Daring Female essence for a spin: Make your vibes spread beyond people you see every day and in more powerful ways. If humor is your secret, set up a Web site and use it to spread your quirky way of looking at life; put a smile on thousands of faces, instead of the dozens that are lucky enough to see you every day. Or write a magazine article/column/book filled with useful advice, bursting with your energy, and work to get it out in front of the world. If you have a special cause you care about, start an organization to promote it, or join an existing organization to fuel it with passion and energy. There are countless ways to let your special assets benefit others; use your Daring Female power to find the one that works best for you. The key is to recognize your own special qualities, have confidence in them, and never shy away from sharing them with others. The world is a better place with you in it, and that's because there's only one you. Enjoy yourself but don't be too selfish and let others enjoy your special qualities as well!

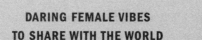

DARING FEMALE VIBES
TO SHARE WITH THE WORLD

- Never-ending energy and the ability to find a way to keep going when it seems there is no way

- Life experience that helps people find their own direction

- A patient ear and the ability to help others sort through their problems and find ways to resolve them

- A sharper-than-a-tack mind able to help anyone turn an idea or desire into an action plan

- Quirky humor that makes even the most serious person break out into laughter

- A positive perspective on the world

- Passion for a cause that infuses others with energy and a desire to take action

- Genuine kindness and generosity

TAKE ON THE DARE

Write down a few of your own special qualities and dare to
share them freely with the world in a direct and assertive
way.

_____

_____

_____

_____

_____

_____

Epilogue
(or Practice What You Preach)

When I started writing this book I was getting through my days on what seemed like pure adrenaline, running off to my job in the morning, coming home at night to work on our publishing business and then on the book, grabbing some food with my husband in between, with maybe half an hour of TV to clear my mind for the next task. It was exhausting and exhilarating, and I'd catch myself thinking that life couldn't get more exhausting or exhilarating than this.

But life has a great way of humbling us just when we think we've got a handle on it. And now I know this first-hand, because by the time I got to editing the first draft of this book I was doing it in semidarkness, as I rocked my one-month-old daughter to sleep in her bouncy seat with my foot. Yep, we had a baby, a beautiful, amazing, incredible baby (is there any other kind?) who came into our lives and taught us what it feels like to be *really* exhausted and exhilarated. Wow, did everything change overnight! Suddenly I was spending every minute of every day thinking about feedings, naps, sleep, feedings, diaper changes, feedings, and lack of sleep. Coming up with new business ideas or working on creative projects couldn't be further from my mind.

After three of the most grueling months I've ever experienced, we exhaled for the first time—cautiously and hesitantly—as we realized that things were getting a bit easier and we and our daughter were learning the ropes of getting through the day without a major tantrum (on her part or ours). That's when I did something I hadn't done in months and went for a walk—by myself, clutching the cell phone in my hand in case my husband had a baby crisis. It felt strange to be out on my own after being attached to my daughter for so long, spending every minute of my day with her. And as I walked, I wondered whether I'd still look at life in the same Daring Female way now that I had a baby to take care of, and the exhaustion and lack of time that came with that responsibility. Would I take as many risks? Would I be as relentless when going after what I wanted out of life? Would I still chase my passions?

I'm still learning about myself as a mom, but I can tell you that being a mom hasn't changed my being a Daring Female. Sure, every action I take and every decision I make is now different because there is a baby in my life. But I still dream and wish and change and take risks and dare to live a full, rich, exciting, and fun life. Nothing will ever change that. I hope that however hectic, busy, and full of responsibility your life is, you won't let it stop you from discovering your inner Daring Female and using every ounce of your Daring Female power to make as much out of every day of your life as possible.

C'mon—I dare you!

Acknowledgments

When I was three years old, I decided to learn how to tie my shoelaces. This was just the latest in the series of steps that I thought were required for me to become completely independent from my parents (it's okay to laugh at this point). I didn't even want them to teach me how to do it. I sat down on a little green bench in the hallway, put on my shoes, and for the next several hours proceeded to figure out how to create loops and tie them together. My parents like to tell this story to illustrate that my independent gene (they mistakenly call it "stubborn") was acting up as much back then as it is now.

It would be tough for me to deny that I am both stubborn and independent, but working on this book has made me realize more than ever that any success or achievement in life is simply not possible without the help, involvement, and hard work of many other people besides myself. And to all the people who have made my life-long dream of becoming a published author possible, I owe you more gratitude than I could ever express.

I'd like to thank my agent, Cathy Fowler, for taking a

chance on an unknown author. The awesome, energetic, and incredibly committed team at Hyperion—and especially my editor, Kiera Hepford—for believing in this book and in me. The dozens of Daring Females whom I interviewed and got to know while working on the book—I could not have done this without you and your inspiring stories.

My thank-yous to my parents could go on for pages, but in this instance, I'd like to thank them for just two things: for bringing me to a country where I can have daring dreams and work my butt off to make them happen and for never getting tired of hearing about my endless ideas, directions, and creative projects.

When I say that this book could not have come to life without my husband, Avi, I mean it in the most genuine way. He was there with me when I came up with the idea, he was the one encouraging me to ignore the pile of rejection letters from my previous interactions with agents and publishers, he was my sounding board as I worked on the book, he was the voice of encouragement and excitement that kept me going through the many, many days when I didn't think I could pull this off. I owe this book to you and I love you.

I should also thank my daughter, Mia, who was born when I was in the middle of writing this book—her smile and even her crying (oh, and did we have some crying!) grounded me in reality and what was truly important in my life, which I realized was not the fact that I could not get a sentence to work from time to time. Thank you, my baby, and thank you for taking your infrequent half-hour naps so that I could run to work on the draft of this book.

Daring Circles

Sometimes there's nothing like a few of your closest friends, fellow reading-group buddies, or trusted colleagues helping you find your inner Daring Female. So here's an idea: Grab a few of them and create your own Daring Circle. Set a time and a place, splurge on some fun food and drinks, and sit in a circle—or as close to it as you can. Turn to the person to your right and dare her to do something that you think will make her life more fun, enjoyable, or fulfilling: quit smoking, start looking for a more rewarding job, start writing that book she is always talking about, end a dead-end relationship, strike up a conversation with the guy she has a crush on, take a yoga class—whatever you think will make her life more ecstatic and will help her find her true inner Daring Female. Agree to meet with your Daring Circle once a week or every couple of weeks and talk about how each of you is doing with your dare. The support and encouragement of your fellow Daring Females, not to mention their helpful suggestions, can do wonders for helping you get out there and make your life what you truly want it to be.

And remember: Sharing is good. Send me an e-mail at natasha@daringfemale.com and tell me about your Daring Circle. If you send me a picture of your Daring Circle, I'll post it on **www.DaringFemale.com** along with your story, so that other Daring Females can find inspiration to create their own Daring Circles.

What's Your Dare?

Visit www.DaringFemale.com and tell me about your dare! Do you dare to finally learn how to ballroom dance? Start writing that book you've always wanted to write? Conquer your fear of public speaking by doing gigs at a comedy club? Whatever it might be, I want to hear about it! Tell me why you want to do it, what it means to you, and what you're doing to make it happen.

And . . .

I'll pick the most gutsy, interesting, creative, unique, and inspiring dares and feature them and their Daring Female creators on my Web site for other Daring Females to see and be inspired by. Each of the featured Daring Females will receive a great-looking Daring Female T-shirt, which comes infused with extra daring energy and entitles the owner to full bragging rights as one of the gutsiest Daring Females out there!